Dr. [...]

DELIVERANCE from SPIRIT HUSBAND and SPIRIT WIFE

(Incubi and Succubi)

Release from Evil Spiritual Marriage

Deliverance From Spirit Husband And Spirit Wife

(Incubi and succubi)

Dr. D. K. Olukoya

ON THE PLAINS OF HESITATION, BLEACH THE BONES OF COUNTLESS MILLIONS WHO, AT THE DAWN OF VICTORY, SAT DOWN TO WAIT, AND WAITING - DIED!

(George W. Cecil [1891-1970])

AFTER READING THIS BOOK, DO NOT HESITATE. TAKE ACTION IMMEDIATELY. YOUR EXISTENCE MAY DEPEND ON IT.

Deliverance From Spirit Husband And Spirit Wife

1st Printing - November, 1999

2nd Printing - October, 2001

ISBN 978-2947-78-4

©1999 The Battle Cry Christian Ministries

All Scripture is from the King James version

Cover illustration by: Mrs. Shade Olukoya

Published by The Battle Cry Christian Ministries
322, Herbert Macaulay Way, Yaba
P. O. Box 12272, Ikeja, Lagos.
Tel. 234 - 8033044239, 01-8044415

Other Publications by Dr. D. K. Olukoya, published and marketed by The Battle Cry Christian Ministries

1. "Adura Agbayori" (Yoruba Version of the Second Edition of Pray Your Way to Breakthroughs).
2. "Awon Adura Ti Nsi Oke Didi" (Yoruba Prayer Book)
3. Be Prepared.
4. Breakthrough Prayers For Business Professionals.
5. Brokenness.
6. Comment Se Delivrer Soi-Meme (French Edition of How To Receive Personal Deliverance).
7. Criminals In The House of God.
8. Dealing With Hidden Curses.
9. Dealing With Unprofitable Roots.
10. Dealing With Witchcraft Barbers.
11. Dealing With Local Satanic Technology.
12. Deliverance By Fire
13. Deliverance Of The Head.
14. Deliverance From Spirit Husband And Spirit Wife.
15. Drawers Of Power From The Heavenlies.
16. Evil Appetite
17. For We Wrestle . . .
18. Fasting And Prayer.
19. Failure In The School Of Prayer.
20. Holy Cry.
21. Holy Fever.
22. How To Obtain Personal Deliverance (Second Edition).
23. Let God Answer By Fire (Annual 70 Days Prayer and Fasting).
24. Limiting God.
25. Meat For Champions.

Other Publications by Dr. D. K. Olukoya, published and marketed by The Battle Cry Christian Ministries

26. Overpowering Witchcraft.
27. Personal Spiritual Check-up.
28. POUVOIR CONTRE LES TERRORISTES SPIRITUELLES (French Edition of Power Against Spiritual Terrorists).
29. Power Against Destiny Quenchers.
30. Power Against Dream Criminals
31. Power Against Local Wickedness.
32. Power Must Change Hands.
33. Power Against Spiritual Terrorists.
34. Power Against Marine Spirits.
35. Power Against Coffin Spirits.
36. Pray Your Way To Breakthroughs (Third Edition).
37. Prayer Rain.
38. Prayer Strategies For Spinsters And Bachelors.
39. Prayers To Destroy Diseases And Infirmities.
40. Prayers that Bring Explosive Increase (Annual 70 Days Prayer and Fasting).
41. Prayers To Mount Up With Wings As Eagles (Annual 70 Days Prayer and Fasting).
42. Prayers that Bring Miracles (Annual 70 Days Prayer and Fasting).
43. Prayers For Open Heaven, New Beginning and Fresh Fire (Annual 70 Days Prayer and Fasting).
44. PRIER JUSQU'A REMPORTER LA VICTOIRE (French Edition of Pray Your Way to Breakthroughs).
45. PRIERES DE PERCEE POUR LES HOMMES D'AFFAIRES (French Edition of Breakthroughs Prayers For Business Professionals).
46. Release From Destructive Covenants.

ALL OBTAINABLE AT:

☞ 11, Gbeto Street, off Iyana Church Bus Stop, Iwaya Road, Iwaya, Yaba, P. O. Box 12272, Ikeja, 0803-304-4239, Lagos, Nigeria.

☞ 15, Olumo Street, Onike, Yaba, Lagos.

☞ 2, Oregun Road, by Radio Bus Stop, Ikeja, Lagos.

☞ MFM Prayer City, KM 12, Lagos/Ibadan Expressway.

☞ 54, Akeju Street, off Shipeolu Street, Palmgrove.

☞ Shop 26, Divine Grace Shopping Plaza, Isolo Jakande Estate, Isolo.

☞ Christian bookstores.

CONTENTS

CHAPTER ONE

There are vicious sexual spirits which can molest and torment susceptible individuals. Sexual spirits that attack females are called incubus and those concentrating on males are called succubus.

An incubus (from the Latin: to lie upon) spirit, is an evil male spirit that lies upon women in their sleep to have intercourse with them. The succubus (from the Latin: to lie under) is a female spirit that comes at night to have sexual relationship with men.

These unclean, familiar spirits may be acquired through sexual promiscuity. They are prominently connected with witchcraft spells, love potions and other curses of lust. They can also operate when people consciously and habitually commit sexual sin. Those coming through heredity cause some of the most terrible problems because they begin their work even on very young children.

The attacks are usually concentrated on the individual while he or she sleeps and he or she may be awakened with fondling hands, caressing hot lips and tongue and other forms of lust inducing stimulation. At first, the affair may seem quite dream-like and the person may even think he or she is imagining things. It can be quite pleasant at the beginning and result in sexual orgasm. However, this is promptly followed by guilt, condemnation and accusation.

Every kind of normal and deviant sexual experience can be generated by these spirits. They delight in inflicting pain, fear and mental anguish on their victims. They stimulate a half-asleep victim to the verge of orgasm, but not allow it. This is to drive the person to masturbation to relieve burning urges and tension.

These depraved spirits play with their captives, cruelly tormenting and using their bodies to satisfy the orgiastic and filthy cravings of the demons. Once entrenched, they do not care whether or not the experience is pleasant for their captive. They prefer that the experience produces pain and suffering. This way they not only enjoy the lust they generate but also the horror with which the cringing and hapless person is filled, as again and again, he is driven to do what he has come to hate and dread. The lower the person can be made to sink, the more animalistic and sickeningly filthy he becomes and the more the demons enjoy their cruel game. Fornication, adultery and any sort of sexual deviation provide opportunity for spirits of sexual lust to operate in one's life.

CHAPTER TWO

Power Against Spiritual Marriages

The problem of spirit husband and spirit wife is one of the greatest problems, which has pervaded all societies of the world.

I had always thought that this problem was restricted to the African environment until white people began to write very touching letters complaining about being harassed by a spirit wife or husband in the dream.

This subject has been grossly neglected for too long. Those who have had problems in this area have decided to keep mute since disclosing their strange experiences is capable of making others view them as strange fellows.

Many people have grappled with bizarre dream experiences that cannot be shared with other people and they have remained under bondage, as no one seems to be able to provide solution to their problems.

Deliverance From Spirit Husband and Spirit Wife

Evil spiritual marriage is real. Many suffer under its yoke and in view of this, I have decided to write this book to thoroughly address the thorny issue.

Many people in Africa and overseas are yearning for solution to problems which emanate from bondage to wicked spiritual spouses. A lot of people are sufficiently aware of the fact that they are involved in an evil marriage which goes beyond the physical realm. Others who are married in the spiritual realm have no inkling that any marriage is in place. Nevertheless, they suffer the consequence. Whichever way we look at it, if you have contracted any marriage with spiritual forces, ignorantly or consciously, the consequences are the same. To be ignorant is to prolong and multiply your suffering. On the other hand, knowledge that is backed up with actions will get you out of the woods, very fast.

You do not have to remain in bondage. You do not have to continue to carry the burdens which spiritual marriage has forced upon you. It is possible to overcome, destroy and paralyse all wicked spiritual spouses. It is possible for you to get to a point where you are able to rid your life of every demonic marital contamination. God knows what you are passing through and it is possible to experience total freedom from every power of darkness that ever got you into an evil marriage.

If you will go through this book, walk in the light of the truth that will be revealed to you, take the prayer points with holy aggression and get to a point where you tell the devil and all spirit wives or husbands that enough is enough, then you will

12

Deliverance From Spirit Husband and Spirit Wife

be free. Marital breakthroughs, release from bondage, peace, progress and stability in every department of life will be your lot.

The subject of spiritual marriage is so important, it goes a long way in determining the kind of life which you will live. It will make a great difference between success and failure in your marriage. Therefore, I challenge you to prepare yourself by taking this important prayer point, take it like a wounded lion:

I challenge all my internal enemies by fire, in the name of Jesus.

May I also state that we are addressing an area which generally angers the devil as he has vowed to keep men and women under bondage. This topic is extremely dangerous and always makes the enemy to frown.

The subject of spirit husband and spirit wife is generally neglected in spiritual warfare literature. A lot of Christians with this problem practise spiritual warfare for years without achieving any tangible result because they did not address and tackle evil spiritual spouses. If you are involved in spiritual marriage, no amount of warfare prayer can lead you to freedom unless you break yourself loose from the evil marriage.

Once a spiritual marriage is in place, evil forces will continue to nullify your prayers on legal grounds. They would tender as exhibits spiritual certificates of marriage in the spiritual court. The moment the exhibits are tendered you remain a victim of evil circumstances. Your evil spiritual husband or wife will continue to control your life. You will be ruled, dominated, abused, manipulated, plundered and dispossessed of every good thing earmarked for you by God.

The chief purpose of the evil spiritual husband or wife is to convert your life to a dustbin or a garbage heap. If you allow him/her to carry out his/her evil activities, your marital, social, business, financial and spiritual life will be in shambles by the time he/she has finished the assignment in your life. Your life will be converted to a trackless wasteland – empty, barren, faded, fallow and totally useless. You might even begin to blame God for what you allowed the devil to do in your life.

Again, the purpose of spirit husband or wife is to get you so confused that you will begin to call your friend your enemy and turn your enemy into your bosom friend. This book has come into your hands as a divine instrument for taking the veil off the face of the enemy. The light of the word of God will cripple the enemy, damage and convert his deadly weapons into harmless toys.

Victory is yours because God is on your side. He has decided to let you into the secrets of the enemy in order to take you from the valley and catapult you to the peak of the mountain. The Bible says: *"And the God of peace shall bruise Satan under your feet shortly. The grace of our Lord Jesus Christ be with you. Amen."* (Romans. 16:20.)

God is aware of what you have suffered at the hands of wicked forces. He has decided to grant you power to

Deliverance From Spirit Husband and Spirit Wife

overcome and exercise dominion over wicked spirits.

Let us meditate on some life-changing truths in the word of God.

That he would grant unto us, that we, being delivered out of the hand of our enemies and might serve him without fear in holiness and righteousness before him, all the days of our life. (Luke 1:74 – 75).

This is an amazing truth, one of the most wonderful eye openers I have found in the word of God. If you are not delivered from the hand of your enemies, you will not be able to serve God without fear. You will be hedged in and hamstrung on all sides by fear. Once your life is filled with fear, your service, as well as your conduct, will be unacceptable to God. The Bible has aptly stated:

Fear has torment and he that feareth is not made perfect (1 John 4:18).

Consequently you will not be able to live a holy life. Your spiritual life will begin to vacillate between high and low and hot and cold points and you will be neither here nor there. You will be hot today but cold tomorrow. You will be happy one moment and despondent the next moment. In one word, your life will be a bundle of contradictions and confusion. The fact that you are under the wicked influence of the enemy will affect you negatively. You will not be able to get the best out of your life. Neither will you be able to chart a course of your own choice. Sinister forces that have vowed to finish you will control you remotely.

At this juncture, I want you to close your eyes and take this crucial prayer point:

Deliverance From Spirit Husband and Spirit Wife

My enemy shall cry for sorrow, in the name of Jesus.

I thank God for His wonderful promise. We shall be delivered out of the hand of our enemies and serve God without fear.

Here is another heart-warning and enlivening promise.

Shall the prey be taken from the mighty, or the lawful captive delivered? But thus saith the LORD, Even the captives of the mighty shall be taken away, and the prey of the terrible shall be delivered: for I will contend with him that contendeth with thee, and I will save thy children. And I will feed them that oppress thee with their own flesh; and they shall be drunken with their own blood, as with sweet wine: and all flesh shall know that I the LORD am thy saviour and thy Redeemer, the MIGHTY one of Jacob (Isa. 49:24-26).

Here is what can be regarded as a million-dollar question that makes the heart to pulsate with anxiety: Shall the prey be taken from the mighty, or the lawful captive delivered? (Isa. 49:24). If rendered, in 21st century English, the question will become, "Is it possible for a deserving culprit, who has gone into bondage, to ever entertain the hope of breathing the air of freedom one day?"

The Bible arouses our consciousness to the fact that some captives deserve the bondage in which they find themselves, hence, the devil has the right to keep them in captivity. Such people are responsible for their own bondage.

Technically, the devil has a legal right to place and keep them in captivity. However, the helpless victims of captivity are promised freedom. The captives of the mighty, as well as the prey of the terrible, shall be delivered. What an amazing promise! Although God has promised us freedom, we should be wary of walking into satanic traps of our own volition. The Bible has left us with very clear indication of the consequences of attracting bondage into our lives. The Bible says:

He that breaketh the hedge the serpent shall bite him (Eccl. 10:8).

I have discovered, from experience as a minister, that most people who are suffering today are completely responsible for what they are going through. Most people who complain are the architects of their misfortune. How do you explain the case of a man who decides to call himself *'Fayemiwo'*. (The *Ifa* oracle or deity has come to conduct an examination over my life.) If that is your name you have decided to send an invitation to the devil to come and examine your life and you must not complain if the result of the examination turns out very bad. Your name has thrown an open invitation to the devil and he is always very quick to grab such an invitation.

Or how would you explain a case of a man whose name is *'Fatimilehin'*, which means that the *Ifa* oracle is my supporter. Such a person must be ready to accept any kind of support from all the powers who are in charge of the *Ifa* oracle.

What comes into your mind when you come across a man whose Yoruba name is *'Sangowanwa'*, meaning *Sango*, the god of thunder, has paid me a visit? If your confession is that an evil deity has visited you, you must be ready to accept whatever it leaves in its travail. Such blind confessions have led many people into bondage.

Other people get into captivity through the violation of the word of God. For example, the Bible says "Thou shall not commit adultery."

If a man who decides to violate God's commandment goes into adultery and becomes infected with the AIDS virus such a person will become a lawful captive.

A woman decides to carry out abortion against the word of God. Immediately she succeeds in terminating the pregnancy, the devil will ensure that she never gets pregnant again. These are examples of lawful captives.

The Bible tells us that all hope is not lost. These lawful captives can and will be delivered if they bring their cases to the court of heaven. There is hope for the hopeless. God is ready to do the impossible to demonstrate His grace, love, and mercy. These captives can repent and cry unto God for mercy and become delivered.

The devil is a legal expert. He is well versed in the laws that govern the spiritual realm. That explains why he has continued to put people into bondage over the ages.

There are two powerful drives in the lives of men and women which the devil has used to trap them and put them in bondage. They are the drives to remain alive and have sex.

The devil has capitalised more on the latter. The devil uses the sexual drive as an instrument for putting people into spiritual prison. Sex can either be legitimate or illegitimate. God has ordained sex as a means of procreation and enjoyment among couples who are legally married. In other words, the only divine platform for sex is marriage. Bible students have discovered that the use of words in the Bible is very instructive.

The Bible has successfully drawn a line between legal and illegal sex. Whenever the Bible describes the type of sex that takes place within the bonds of marriage the words are always specific, "Knew his wife," but when sex takes place outside marriage the Bible says something like, "And a man laid with her." Therefore, we know that "To lie with a woman" is to have sex outside marriage while "To know a woman" means to have sex with your own wife. Any sex outside marriage opens you up to an invasion from the pit of hell. Such a sinful act will construct a bad platform or foundation for your marriage.

Unknown to most people, most of the problems they are going through came into their lives through illicit sexual relationship. If you are a woman, you must know this, your womb as well as your virginity has a gate. Whoever breaks your virginity has a great spiritual impact on your life and future. When you allow a man to defile you, you have formed a very powerful covenant with him. The moment your blood comes in contact with the man's organ you have entered a very powerful covenant with him.

This fact must be made very plain, because there are many ladies who are going through mysterious situations. Such ladies have tried positive confession, prayer and fasting, consultation with prophets and many men of God and other effective means of procuring solutions to knotty problems. Unfortunately, these methods have proved abortive. If you

Deliverance From Spirit Husband and Spirit Wife

visit a doctor and you complain that your stomach is aching when your real problem is that you have caught a fever the doctor may likely prescribe a wrong medication unless he runs you through proper medical diagnosis.

In the same vein, if your problem is rooted in the fact that spiritual spouses have put your life on hold, trying to solve the problem without knowing the cause, will amount to chasing shadows.

Our approach differs significantly from that of others. When I address spiritual problems, I go beyond the surface, to the very root. A tree stands because its roots are firmly fixed to the ground. Even if you cut a tree, it might sprout again after sometime. If you succeed in uprooting it, you have succeeded in dealing a permanent blow on the tree.

It is a common knowledge that experts are in high demand in every sphere of life. It is very easy to follow the bandwagon. But it is a mark of excellence to approach the particular matter in a way that makes you stand out.

Spiritual warfare is a unique subject. There are Christians and there are Christians, just as there are soldiers and there are soldiers. A private in the army is a soldier, while the general is also a soldier. But what a general can do a private cannot do. Some soldiers have never fought any battle. There are soldiers who are motor drivers, music players, school teachers and aides to senior officers. Although these categories of soldiers are in the national army, they are far from being trusted in the act of warfare. When there is a civil or external war, only combatant soldiers are called into the scene. They are the real soldiers.

With all humility, I want to declare that trained members of the Mountain of Fire and Miracles Ministries belong to the class of combatant spiritual soldiers. Other believers may decide to live like civilians in army uniform, but the kind of end-time believers which God had mandated me to raise up, cannot afford the luxury of living carelessly in the battle field.

We sometimes appear strait-laced to many, for we have chosen to be different, since we are aware of the peculiarity of the end-times. For example, we often tell some ladies to do away with strange hair which they attach to their natural hair because such products emanate from the domain of the queen of the coast. Such ladies generally argue with us simply because they know nothing about the appearance of the queen of the coast. They argue with us because spiritual warfare sounds like Greek to their ears.

If a man of God who has confronted the queen of the coast tells you to remove the strange embellishments with which you adorn yourself and you choose to disobey him, you are toying with a spiritual scorpion. It will bite sooner or later. The price you will pay will far outweigh all anticipated gains. This shows that many churches are peopled with 'ice-cream' soldiers. If you correct such people, they pout and weep like babies who are toying with the tail of a scorpion.

The greatest good you can do to yourself is to get enlisted in a school of combatant soldiers. We have witnessed more

Deliverance From Spirit Husband and Spirit Wife

insurrections, uproars, battles, invasions and deadly attacks in this generation than in any other past generation. Every Christian who is worth his salt should portray the character of a rugged combatant soldier. To do otherwise is to close your eyes and walk into a satanic trap.

Those who have fought in a battle field know that it is dangerous to stay like a civilian in the face of enemy fire. A soldier who is conscious of the perils of warfare would be on the alert every second. Some soldiers have spent hours, days and weeks staying awake in order to avert danger. If that can be done because of physical warfare, how much more should we gird our loins in order to win in the battles of life which are spiritual.

You must therefore discard your old ideas, temperament, comportment and lifestyle and receive some spiritual drills. You must devote ample time and energy to spiritual training. The more training you receive, the more victory you receive. The more rank you acquire the more your ability to exercise dominion over the devil.

If Christians can just devote more time to spiritual war, there will be more peace, prosperity, stability and progress in Christian homes. Training in spiritual warfare is the need of the hour. If you dare to become a combatant soldier, the devil will bow down before you. The enemy will take his hands off your marriage. Your marriage will become a success story.

THE FOUNDATION

Great problems begin as insignificant issues. When such issues are multiplied, the result can be imagined.

Let us examine some issues that are often overlooked in the modern age:

The first born dilemma - The first born dilemma is perhaps the most enigmatic phenomenon in the African society. When a family gives birth to the first baby, a lot of things are done. These include consultation with fetish priests and soothsayers, sacrifices, dedication to family idols, performing of rituals, etc.

The first born in many families have built their lives on the foundation of evil actions. Unknown to them, what their parents have done is capable of placing them inside evil cages.

When a family is under a curse, the first child will come into the world with extra evil luggage upon his head. As the first one to go through the open gate, he is very likely to gather all kinds of evil cobwebs on his head. This is why we often discover that the first one in a family generally has more problems than other children in the family. He is used as the sacrificial lamb. By the time the second, the third and the fourth are born, the evil family luggage would have been borne by the first child on their behalf.

Committing immorality with prostitutes - This is another foundational problem. If a man commits immorality with a prostitute, he has opted for the greatest bondage that can be imagined. The moment the man commits sin with a prostitute, demons from the last seven men who had sex with the prostitute automatically gain entrance into his life. Such a man will not be short of what can be described as multiple bondage. Also all the spirit husbands of the prostitute would begin to harass him because he is sleeping with their wife.

Sexual Immorality - Sexual immorality is a serious foundational problem. The moment you have sex with someone you are not married to, you have invited problem into your life.

Bachelors and spinsters who commit immorality are digging their own graves. A Christian sister who commits immorality with a man who is loose sexually invites problems into her own life. Such a Christian sister can sing like a nightingale, she is simply not born again. If a Christian sister decides to give her body to a so-called Christian brother, she is building her marriage on a weak platform. If she continues with such a relationship, she would soon discover that the man messes up with other ladies the way he messes up with her.

If a lady sleeps with a loose man, demons from the last seven women whom he slept with will enter into her. That is exactly how many people enter into bondage.

Rites of protection - Many people enter bondage as a result of rites of protection performed for their well-being and security by their parents. Perhaps your parents had a hard time bearing children and decided to consult some local fetish priests, fringe prophets, occult practitioners, diviners and people who lay claim to the ability to keep children who are fond of dying each time they are born.

If your parents went to consult voodoo priests who specialise in taming 'Abiku' or 'Ogbanje' (children who have supposedly gone through various cycles of existence) they have given out your hand in marriage to spiritual powers.

If a sp rit accepts the responsibility of protecting you or preventing you from being harmed by hostile powers, that superior spirit will likely contract a marriage with you. That may be your own way of paying an evil fee.

Cultural dances - A lot of people have entered into demonic marriages through participation in cultural dances. Perhaps you got involved with cultural dances when you were very young, you may have been married to some gods or goddesses. In some African communities, young ladies are almost naked when they perform traditional dances. Some people even go ahead to declare that they are getting married to demonic deities

Sexual perversion - Sexual perversion constitutes a very strong entry point for wicked spirit husbands and wives. Any sexual relationship that violates the word of God leads to an evil spiritual marriage. Fornication, adultery, incest, masturbation, lesbianism, homosexuality, bestiality, pornography and prostitution are avenues for getting into marriage with spirit husbands and wives.

This generation has seen the worst sexual perversion. If

25 .

you read the daily, the paper's increasing number of bizarre
s incidents of sexual perversion will shock you.

Some African ladies have become so demonic that they
travel to far away Europe where they allow dogs and other
animals sleep with them for a fee. Those who are involved in
such horrific abominations will obviously get married to
terrible wicked spirit husbands.

Ladies who give away their womanhood to demonic dogs
would receive marriage invitations from multiple wicked
spirits. If a man eventually sleeps with such ladies, he will be
in trouble. The spirits that came into such a woman through
sexual perversion (bestiality) will invade the life of the man.

Sexual perversion includes sexual flashbacks, flirting,
seduction, petting, kissing, inordinate affection, oral sex and
looking lustfully at women. These practices open the door for
spirit husbands and wives to come in.

Indecent dressing - Those who put on any dress that
violates the principles of Christian dressing are responsible for
inviting spirit husbands or wives. Demonic spirits introduce
majority of the styles that are prevalent today. If you copy
such styles, you will bag a spirit husband or wife.

Why should a so-called Christian lady or indeed any lady
put on a gown that makes her look like a mermaid or a fish.
If a lady dresses seductively, it is an indication of the fact that
she is looking for a wicked spirit husband.

Dresses that make a lady to wriggle her body like a snake
are part of invitation to evil spiritual marriage.

Deliverance From Spirit Husband and Spirit Wife

Ladies who style their hair or put artificial attachments to it to make them look like the queen of the coast, will get attached to a spirit husband faster than they can ever imagine.

Do you know that some of the women's adornments can attract human beings and spirits?

If you are a sister and you have vowed never to give up your trousers, you have simply made up your mind to offer yourself in marriage to demonic husbands.

SATANIC STRATEGY

Let us at this point examine how the devil has succeeded in perverting sex, using it as a weapon of spiritual slavery.

Sex is ordained by God for living things like human beings and animals. What comes to your mind when you know that spirits are trying to get into you through that realm? Why should spirit beings veer into sex? Why are evil spirits bent on having canal knowledge of men and women? Can they go into such an act without having any purpose at the back of their minds?

Let us examine the Scriptures:

For this cause shall a man leave his father and mother, and shall be joined unto his wife, and they two shall be one flesh. This is a great mystery: but I speak concerning Christ and the church (Ephesians 5:31-32)

The revelation in the passage you have just read is that sexual intimacy is a mystery. It defies human logic. It is a spiritual action. When two people come together sexually,

27

both become one flesh. It can either be positive or negative.

When you have sex with a particular person, you become one flesh, spiritually speaking. This unity can either be a blessing or a curse. If you sleep with your wife, you become one with her in a positive sense. But if you sleep with anybody besides your wife, you become one with such a fellow in a terribly negative sense. This fact is corroborated by another passage:

Know ye not that your bodies are the members of Christ? Shall I then take the members of Christ, and make them the members of an harlot? God forbid. What? Know ye not that he which is joined to an harlot is one body? For two, saith he, shall be one flesh. But he that is joined unto the Lord is one spirit. Flee fornication. Every sin that a man doeth is without the body; but he that committeth fornication sinneth against his own body. What? Know ye not that your body is the temple of the Holy Ghost which is in you, which ye have of God, and ye are not your own? For ye are bought with a price: therefore glorify God in your body, and in your spirit, which are God's (I Corinthians 6:15-20).

Paul, the apostle, a man who was divinely endowed with insight into spiritual mysteries, gives us an eye opener into the mysteries of sex. The above passage suggests that Paul wondered why Christians in his days lacked proper knowledge concerning the spiritual realities behind sex. Twice he queried: "What? Know ye not" in six short verses. He expected them to know that sex goes beyond physical enjoyment.

Sex is a covenant. It is a deeply spiritual act capable of enslaving forever those who blindly go into it illegally. I am deeply saddened by the fact that many people are completely ignorant of the fact that there is a spiritual mystery behind sex.

A single act of sex is capable of joining your body, your soul and your spirit with that of another, regardless of who the person is. Modern day believers may be ignorant of this fact, but satan and his demons are not. They are sufficiently aware of what takes place during sexual intercourse. That is why they have continuously used it as an evil weapon of dragging careless men or women into deep bondage.

Sex is so powerful that it unites the spirit and soul. The power of sex is so awesome that the devil has chosen it as his chief instrument. The only other thing that has this kind of power is the blood covenant. This explains why men often find it difficult to break away from certain relationships. How can you break away from a relationship when you are involved in something that is spiritual in nature? Even if you take physical actions, the powers behind the mystery of sex will not release you.

Sleeping with many partners will end up fragmenting your soul. I do not make this statement to frighten you. Many lives are fragmented because they have shared their bodies, souls and spirits with multiple sex partners. Such people will never be able to hold themselves together except they go through deliverance.

A lot of people have sold their virtues and prosperity through involvement with spirit husbands, or wives. Just as marriage is a covenant that binds two people together, sex is also capable of binding two partners. Anyone who wants to continue committing immorality should be ready to pay the price of becoming fragmented.

Therefore, when an evil spirit decides to lead people into bondage, it attacks such victims by abusing them sexually. The moment a spirit wife or husband succeeds in having sex with you in your dream, you are automatically joined with that wicked spirit. Your life will become fragmented. The better part of your life, virtue, goodness and prospects will be kept in a demonic bank. You will not be able to make progress physically, since your virtues have been stolen and deposited under an evil altar.

You will put up a lot of actions without achieving any result. That is not the only price to pay. You may even experience untimely death. Before that happens, you would have contracted a spiritual marriage with the spirit. You will suffer the consequences of evil marriage without being able to trace it to sex dreams.

Wicked spirit husbands and wives have one goal, to pollute the life of the victim. Demonic spouses operate like mosquitoes, they spread evil viruses, that is why we call them spiritual rapists. They attack their victims when they know that resistance or refusal is possible. They normally carry out their survey or research in an intelligent manner.

The question which normally comes up in their mindS is how they can make the fellow a candidate of spiritual bondage or how they can pollute the fellow's life. Of course, the answer is clear: introduction of spiritual sex. Here lies 90

Deliverance From Spirit Husband and Spirit Wife

percent of the problems of marriage which spinsters, bachelors and married people have.

The Bible states that the spirit of man is the candle of the Lord. Your light cannot burn bright except there is a link between your spirit and the Spirit of God. The devil knows that your spirit is very important. That is why he has released myriads of candle polluters into the world. These spirits have continued to obey their master, the devil. They are ready to pollute as many lives as possible. That is why you must command these wicked spirits to release the candle, of your life. If you allow them to pollute your candle, the totality of your life will be polluted.

The existence of spirit wives and spirit husbands is neither a fantasy nor a fairy tale. It is as real as the air you breathe.

Spirit wives and husbands hate the institution of marriage with perfect hatred. They can be classified into a number of categories:

Physical spiritual spouses - Some wicked spiritual spouses operate physically. Some of their victims can actually see them. I have come across victims who suffer demonic sexual harassment while they are wide-awake. They become sexually excited when there is no living soul around them. The enemy is using that wicked device to destroy many lives.

A lot of people have not been able to get married because of such abnormal experience.

Wicked spiritual spouses whose victims are either conscious or unconscious - Victims of demonic sexual harassment can also be divided into two categories. Some are conscious while others are unconscious. However, I have discovered that majority who are visited by spirit husbands and wives are unconscious of what is happening to them.

To be precise, more than 90 percent are unconscious victims of this sexual exploitation and abuse. Evil spirits are bent on keeping their victims in the dungeon of ignorance. They do not want their victims to come to the knowledge of the fact that they are attacking them.

Spiritual prostitutes - Another category of spiritual wives and husbands is the company of spiritual prostitutes. These spiritual prostitutes do not limit themselves to one victim. They attack as many people as possible. The more people they attack the more havoc they cause.

Wandering spirits - Some wicked spirit husbands and wives are mandated to wander from one victim to another. Such spirits can operate in many continents. They multiply the demonic bondage from nation to nation.

Spiritual twins - These wicked spirit husbands and wives operate like physical twins. They carry out their activities with their evil twin brother or sister.

Wicked and violent spirit - This category of spirit is violent when they sexually abuse their victims. I have come across victims who wake up with excruciating pain in their reproductive organs immediately they are roused from a sex dream.

Some ladies have gone through traumatic experiences just

because some spirit husbands have violently abused them sexually. Such ladies feel the pain in real life. Some men have come to me to narrate how they woke up in the morning with violent pains in their private parts.

Masquerade or camouflage spirit - This category of spirit often takes up the appearance of someone who their victims would hardly reject. When an evil spiritual spouse comes in the appearance of someone you are fond of, you may not resist such an advance. Many people have been sexually abused not knowing that evil spirits hid under the facial appearance of a loved one.

Family spirit husbands or wives - It may sound strange to the ignorant that some families have spirit husbands or wives. Such personalities generally marry every member of that family. The evil spouses generally have sex spiritually with every member of the family, thereby enslaving them.

Resident spiritual husbands or wives - Many people unconsciously harbour evil spouses within them. Immediately they close their eyes the evil spouses come out and begin to abuse them.

Hermaphrodite spirit - This spirit comes against its victims with both male and female organs. The spirit has different functions and attacks different victims.

ACTIVITIES OF THE WICKED SPIRITS

What then are the activities of these wicked spirits?

Satanic initiation - These spirits initiate their victims.

Deliverance From Spirit Husband and Spirit Wife

Immediately spirit wives or husbands succeed in having sex with a man or woman, initiation is carried out.

Destruction of virtues - Evil spouses generally destroy the virtues of anyone they have sex with. If the victim is destined to succeed, they destroy his potentials through spiritual sex.

A lot of people have confided in me saying, "Dr. I don't know why this happens to me every time, whenever I am about to start a big project, or I am going for an interview, an evil spouse appears to me in the dream and harasses me sexually." The results of such evil dreams have continued to baffle me.

Sex dreams always portend failure, calamity and non-achievement.

Siphoning the power of God - These wicked spirits use the weapon of spiritual sex to siphon the power of God in the lives of the victims. A lot of people who are anointed by God have lost their power through being sexually abused by spirit wives and husbands. Whenever an evil personality succeeds in luring you to sex in the dream, you will wake up the next day feeling empty spiritually.

Late marriages - One of the wicked activities of these evil personalities is the programming of late marriages into the lives of their victims. If you examine the lives of men and women, who are visited regularly by spirit husbands or wives you will discover that most of them generally end up getting married either when they are almost near or have passed their prime age. Such people come across many potential

34

partners, but each proposal ends up in the rain.

Some people would never have got married if they had not gone through deliverance. Even when some people get married, evil spiritual spouses still attempt to make them childless.

Misfortune - Misfortune is the stock in trade of evil spiritual spouses. They cause as many misfortunes as possible in the lives of their victims.

Profitless hard-work - Wicked spiritual spouses may allow you to work your fingers to the bone. But they will not allow you to make profit. They will allow you to initiate and execute many projects, but they will not allow you to reap the fruits of your labour.

While many will commend your assiduity and zeal, demonic powers will not allow you to experience or attain success.

Marital confusion - Wicked spiritual spouses inject confusion into the family lives of their victims. When such people discover the will of God in their lives, they slump into confusion as soon as they have a sex dream.

Somebody came up saying, "Pastor, God gave me a very clear revelation. God has led me to get married to sister Jane. I am as sure of the revelation as I am of my salvation. I saw sister Jane's face seven times, Pastor, please give us a go-ahead to get married."

A month later, the same fellow came back saying, "Pastor, I am sorry to bother you, I feel somewhat confused. I think I

Deliverance From Spirit Husband and Spirit Wife

made a mistake when I spoke to you about sister Jane. God has given me another revelation. I believe God wants me to marry sister Martha. Just last night, in a dream, I saw both of us at the altar, putting on wedding garments. I can hardly wait to see the marriage consummated." Confusion!

These wicked spiritual spouses lead their victims into other types of confusion. I have heard of the cases of those who died exactly a week to the date of their marriage. Some go into a big fight during their courtship and their marriage plans crash like a pack of cards. We often hear of people who are in courtship for months coming up with a decision to break up the relationship. Why does such a thing happen?

A woman suddenly woke up one morning and found herself hating the man she had loved dearly. The man became so odious that she was not willing to set her eyes on him. The woman succeeded in calling it quit with the man before she realised that she had been manipulated by a wicked spirit husband. She may start a new relationship with another man with a smooth beginning but sooner or later the relationship will turn sour.

The spirit of hatred, occasioned and energised by her spirit husband will make it impossible for her to achieve stability in her relationships.

Many men have gained mastery in the art of postponing their wedding. Today, they tell everyone that they are going to get married this year, it never materialises. Tomorrow, they go ahead to inform the brethren that they are going to get married. The following year, it never happens. They postpone wedding dates every year, till nobody believes them. The spirit of confusion trails them.

I have seen extremely beautiful ladies who are successful in their profession but are dejected because they cannot make up their minds in the area of marriage. I have also come across extremely handsome gentlemen who cannot get married.

I know a particular sister who tried several times to get married but failed at each attempt. She had a strange experience each time she announced her wedding date. Whenever it was exactly two weeks to the date, some stubborn and ugly pimples would develop on her face. Each man was very ashamed to take her to the altar. That was how all the men that promised to marry her withdrew.

The activities of a spirit husband or wife can hardly be completely enumerated. Most Caesarean operations which take place in the hospitals are the handiwork of spirit husbands. Do you know what they say to such victims? "You escaped our trap and you want to get married and raise children successfully. We are going to give you the toughest fight of your life. Go ahead and get pregnant, we are going to cause you to have a Caesarean operation and you will not survive it. You cannot give birth to children in the spiritual realm and also raise children in real life."

What a wicked threat!

Deliverance From Spirit Husband and Spirit Wife
THE DIVINE SOLUTION - STEPS TO VICTORY

Are you afraid of what you have read so far? Do you dread the activities of wicked spiritual spouses? Have you concluded that it is impossible to experience freedom from their wicked activities?

May I tell you this?: the devil is wicked but God is good. The devil is a nonentity as far as God is concerned. God has a solution for every problem engineered by the devil and his lieutenants. Are you suffering from the hands of wicked spirit husband or wife?

God has a solution for your trials and travails. God's intention is that marriage should be limited to the physical realm. Relationships between human beings and spirits are gross violations of the decision of God.

Through wicked manipulation, satan has corrupted normal human relationships. He has led countless number of souls into terrible bondage by getting them involved in spiritual sexual relationships which they know nothing about. This is the bedrock of mankind's problems.

Anyone who has sexual intercourse in the dream is under serious satanic bondage. To make matters worse, some people even get pregnant and are delivered of children in the dreams. These instances will make it impossible for them to achieve success and stability in their marriage.

Are you ready to receive a divine solution from the Lord? Briefly stated here are the steps to victory.

Repentance - You must repent wholeheartedly. God.

expects you to cry unto Him in repentance as soon as you have identified the satanic doorway that have introduced spirit husbands or wives into your life. You must be specific, practical and painstaking as you go to God in total repentance. You must be able to mention the names of all the persons that you have slept with and repent of every sinful act. You must rely on the Holy Spirit to remind you of all sinful relationships.

Return and destroy illegally acquired gifts - Many people received gifts from their sinful partners without thinking about the consequences of receiving such gifts. Many people have gone into bondage by receiving gifts through relationships that they went into.

If you received a gift from a demonic man or woman, spirit husbands or wives have the right to visit and molest you sexually. If a particular man bought things like wrist watches, towel, under wear, gift items, drugs and dresses for a lady, the lady is expected to do away with such gifts, since she knows the relationship is no longer valid. If you decide to continue to use such items, they will reinforce the powers of spirit husbands.

Plead the blood of Jesus - The blood of Jesus is such a terrific weapon that is capable of dislodging or evicting spirit husbands or wives from the territory of your life. Issue quit notice to all illegal tenants by pleading the blood of Jesus.

Renounce the marriage - You must specifically renounce all vows or agreement made with spirit husbands or wives.

Deliverance From Spirit Husband and Spirit Wife

You must order them to pack their loads and depart from you and never to return. Let me give you some scriptures, which you can use to renounce an evil marriage:

Jesus answered and said unto them, Ye do err, not knowing the scriptures, nor the power of God. For in the resurrection they neither marry, nor are given in marriage, but are as the angels of God in heaven (Matthew 22:29,30).

On the basis of this, you can enforce your legal right by telling spirit husband or wife that spirits are forbidden from getting married. Let me give you another passage which can be used as a weapon against evil spouses.

Ye shall keep my statutes. Thou shalt not let thy cattle gender with a diverse kind: thou shalt not sow thy field with mingled seed: neither shall a garment mingled of linen and woollen come upon thee (Leviticus 19:19).

The second arrow which you can send to the camp of wicked spiritual husbands or wives who are hell-bent on molesting you sexually is that God forbids any form of gender with diverse kind. Therefore, God forbids them sexual intercourse with human beings.

Deuteronomy 25:14 also says:

Thou shalt not have in thine house divers measures, a great and a small.

God forbids diverse measures. Hence He cannot allow spirit beings and human beings to mix together. If you are a child of God, you must be able to tell this to the devil. The Bible makes us to know that if one of the partners in a marriage is dead, the second is free. Tell the devil I am dead in Christ and I can no longer be married to you.

Deliverance From Spirit Husband and Spirit Wife

💰 Any form of marital relationship with you is broken according to Romans 7:1-4:

Know ye not, brethren, (for I speak to them that know the law,) how that the law hath dominion over a man as long as he liveth? For the woman which hath an husband is bound by the law to her husband so long as he liveth; but if the husband be dead, she is loosed from the law of her husbands. So then if, while her husband liveth, she be married to another man, she shall be called an adulteress, though she be married to another man. Wherefore, my brethren, ye also are become dead to the law by the body of Christ; that ye should be married to another, even to him who is raised from the dead, that we should bring forth fruit unto God.

Additionally, you can use II Corinthian 11:2,3:

For I am jealous over you with godly jealousy: for I have espoused you to one husband, that I may present you as a chaste virgin to Christ. But I fear, lest by any means, as the serpent beguiled Eve through his subtilty, so your minds should be corrupted from the simplicity that is in Christ.

You must declare before the company of evil spouses that you are married to Jesus who is jealous over you with godly jealousy. Finally, you can turn Deuteronomy 24:1-4 into a battle axe.

When a man hath taken a wife, and married her, and it come to pass that she find no favour in his eyes, because he hath found some uncleanness in her: then let him write her a bill of divorcement, and give it in her hand, and send her out of his house. And when she is departed out of his house, she may go and be another man's *wife*. And *if* the latter husband hate her, and write her a bill of divorcement, and giveth it in her hand, and sendeth her out of his house; or if the latter husband die, which took her to *be* his wife; Her former husband, which sent her away, may not take her again to be his wife, after that she is defiled; for that *is* abomination before the Lord: and thou shalt not cause the land to sin, which the Lord thy God giveth thee *for* an inheritance.

The import of this passage is that you must rise up and issue a certificate of divorcement to all wicked spirit husbands and wives.

Go and sin no more - The last step which God expects you to take is that you must say bye-bye to sin and the devil. Continue to live a holy life and the devil will never succeed in leading you into an evil marriage.

Finally, I appeal to you to make up your mind to pray fervently. Most people who are battling with the problem of evil spouses have not prayed to a point to discover their true spiritual identity. I want you to learn a lesson from the life of Prophet Isaiah. The prophet preached fire and brimstone in the first chapter. In the second chapter, he comes up with proclamation of fiery judgement. He begins to talk tough in the third chapter. He begins to spit fire in chapter four. He emits an acidic prophecy in the fifth chapter.

The sixth chapter introduces a new dimension into the biography of the respected man of God. We suddenly discover that prophet Isaiah had a long way to go . He saw the Lord and the story changed. He saw the Lord and his opinion about himself changed. He declared, "Woe unto me, I am a man of unclean lips." The angel of the Lord dropped fire on Isaiah's lips and he began to see the Lord. He began to talk about the Messiah.

Serious Bible students have agreement on the fact that reading from the sixth chapter to the end of the book of

Deliverance From Spirit Husband and Spirit Wife

Isaiah, is like reading the New Testament. Isaiah is regarded as the evangelist of the Old Testament. He saw the Lord and was never the same again. Today, I challenge you to pray until God gives you a vision that will change your life.

CHAPTER THREE

Foundations of Marital Distress

The prevailing situation of the modern age points to the fact that this is the age of marital distress. It goes without saying that many marriages are sick to the point of death. In fact, many couples have already packed up their marriages. Several men and women are exploring new ways of achieving satisfaction in life as they know that they have failed woefully in their marital lives.

Some successful businessmen, highly-rated professionals, technocrats, renowned politicians and men who seem to have made their mark in the world are not finding the same level of success in marriage. Nine out of ten people are actually suffering from marital distress. The situation leaves much to be desired. The situation has continued to bother me as I survey the marital situation in the nation and in the church. If God's people are experiencing marital distress, what is the fate of the ungodly?

Deliverance From Spirit Husband and Spirit Wife

If Christians are finding it hard to achieve peace, stability and success in their marriages, what is the hope of those who have no relationship with God? We cannot afford to gloss over an issue as weighty as the institution of marriage. We must get down to the foundation and address this knotty issue. The moment we are able to discover the root of marital distress, we are sure of receiving divine help, which will, consequently, turn our marital situation around.

We need the wisdom of the Ancient of days. Our wisdom will fail us. Our skills may not suffice. My scientific and academic training has made me to know that erudition and human logic cannot hold the home together. There are renowned professors of psychology who, are divorcees. I wonder what has happened to their knowledge of psychology? Why can't they bring psychological theories to bear on their marriage? Why are they so sound in human and animal psychology but they do not know how to relate with women who have no academic degrees. If some of these academic professors are sincere, they should seek for genuine help. How true are the words of the Bible?

"Great men are not always wise. Neither do the aged understand" **(Job 32:9).**

Therefore, the greatest problem anyone can ever have is to refuse to seek help from the Almighty. Solution to marital distress begins with definite steps towards bringing God into your marital situation. No marital distress is so acute that it cannot be taken care of by God. Perhaps your marital situation is a far cry from what you anticipated several years

45

ago. Perhaps you have actually come to your wit's end. It is also possible that you have decided to throw in the towel. Who knows, you might have vowed that you would never have anything to do with marriage again.

May I offer you some prophetic words of encouragement. Your situation will not remain the same. God will turn it around. Man's extremity, they say, is God's opportunity. What has been stumbling blocks before you will soon become stepping-stones to marital success. Although you might have found yourself in the throes of marital distress, that kind of situation will not last forever.

A lot of people whose marital lives have become models of excellence started out with problems that they never thought about. I have discovered that a lot of people who have distress in their marital lives have potentials for achieving great exploits in marriage. The only problem is that they are ignorant of these potentials. Therefore, many of them have given up when they are supposed to make a little more effort in order to draw upon the grace and the power of God. If you are ready to receive divine help, your travails in the area of marriage will become a thing of the past. God will turn your marital distress to miracles, and your testimony will be an encouragement to a multitude.

Beloved, I want you to manifest violent faith in the Lord. Violent faith is the faith that has no patience with the enemy. It is sad that many people have lost every sense of direction in the area of marriage.

Deliverance From Spirit Husband and Spirit Wife

A lot of people are being pushed back and forth by powers beyond them. Some who are expected to have broken new grounds in every department of marital life are still struggling to get started. Many people have lost money, position and wonderful opportunities when they are expected to come up with unprecedented records of achievements.

A lot of people are confused having met their enemies in every corner, enemies attack them in their business, family and social lives. It is possible that what I have said so far has aptly described your situation. It is possible that you have the feeling of being surrounded by terrible enemies.

There is no gainsaying the fact that you know that God has something wonderful in store for you, but the problem is that you have found it difficult to reconcile your daily experiences with the good things, which you have continued to anticipate. I know that you have good dreams about the present and the future. I know that you are ready to pay the price of outstanding success and achievement in life. It is even possible that you have tried your best without any tangible result. I know that you have waited for the manifestation or fulfilment of the promises of God for quite sometime now.

I also know that it is possible you are tired of waiting for your miracles. I have no doubt in my heart concerning the fact that you have tried every method that you know. I know that you are willing to go beyond your present level in life. The fact that you are reading this book means you are ready to receive help. Do not be intimidated by the fact that your previous attempt to solve life's problems in general and marital

Deliverance From Spirit Husband and Spirit Wife
problems in particular did not yield the kind of result you desired. Just take one more step and your miracle is sure.

My heart goes out to those who are hurting. I am burdened for men and women who know that their present position in life is far away from where God wants them to be. I am praying with all my heart for those who have continuously found it difficult to attain their dreams, hopes and aspirations in life.

A lot of people are simply confused; they do not understand themselves. When such people are alone, they ask themselves questions like "What is wrong with me? What is happening to me? I have prayed, gone through deliverance, made several positive confessions and attended many Christian programmes, why am I still suffering? Why is nothing working for me? Why?" The greatest problem, which any man can go through in life is that of marital distress. It is easier to cope with business distress than to cope with marital distress.

However, 1 have discovered that most marital distresses which people suffer from have their roots in a deeper evil. Those who suffer marital distress do not know that evil powers are actually aiming at the lives. They are attacking their victim's marital lives only as part of a grand plan to get rid of them. Wicked satanic agents are actually bent on eliminating most people who are complaining that they are suffering from marital distress. Yes, 1 know that your marital life is under attack, but that is not the end of the story. The devil and his agents are actually gunning for your life. That is why I want you to be angry with the devil. You must get to a point where you are willing to talk back to the devil and say Enough is enough.

I am aware of the fact that some people are fighting, a battle when they go to bed. Many people are restless because they sense the enemy's attack from day to day. Why should your life be converted to a battleground when Jesus said:

Come unto me, all ye that labour and are heavy laden, and I will give you rest. Take my yoke upon you, and learn of me; for I am meek and lowly in heart; and ye shall find rest unto your souls. For my yoke is easy, and my burden is light (Matthew 11:28-30).

Why should you claim to be a believer when rest is foreign to you? Why must you allow the devil to render the word of God of no effect in your life? God will change your situation. He is going to deal with your enemies and make them to bow before you. You are going to experience the power of God today. It is possible that you have become an object of ridicule, simply because your marital life has been turned upside down by the devil. Now is the time for you to ask the God of Elijah to stand up on your behalf.

Get ready for divine visitation as you take these prayer points. Please, lay your right hand on your head as you pray with holy madness:

Every witchcraft arrow, come out by fire, in the name of Jesus.

Every satanic twin sister/brother that is collecting my blessings fall down and die, in the name of Jesus.

The Bibles says;

Deliverance From Spirit Husband and Spirit Wife

If the foundations be destroyed, what can the righteous do? (Psalm 11:3).

The foundation of a building plays a crucial role in its stability. If it is faulty, the structure on it will not stand. Most of us who live in this generation are fortunate when compared with our ancestors. Many of the things which we address today were not addressed in those days.

If you talk with those who got married 50 or 60 years ago they would tell you that most of their problems can be traced to lack of opportunities. It is quite possible that your parents did not have access to the facts which you are reading today. Your parents would have been happier if they had had a good opportunity to lay a solid foundation for their homes. Many of them suffered because they did not have pastors or believers around them. You have the opportunity of laying a good foundation. Today, you have the opportunity of dealing with any enemy that wants to fight against your marriage.

If you are single, you can use the weapon of prayer as a tool for getting the right partner for your life. You have the opportunity of breaking yourself loose from all chains, which have put you into collective captivity. If you are able to clear a lot of things from your background, you will succeed in getting rid of problems that will arise later in life.

LESSONS FROM CREATION

The foundation of everything in life is very important. We have a lot of lessons to learn from the story of creation. The book of Genesis shows us the process of creation. God created the world and He also created man. However, a crucial step was taken in Genesis when God created a woman. The Bible throws light on how God instituted the first marriage in Genesis 2:18:

And the Lord God said, It is not good that the man should be alone; I will make him an help meet for him.

God places a great premium on marriage. Your marriage is more important to God than you can ever imagine. God does not expect you to joke with your marriage. He actually states that it is not good for a man to be alone, neither is it good for a woman to be alone. Marriage is not an accident. Neither is it a pass time, it is a matter of life and death. Marriage cannot be compared with a commuter bus that you can board and get off at will.

Once you board the vehicle of marriage, you are expected to remain on board, no matter what happens. You can jump into marriage, but you cannot jump out of it. It is easy to rush into marriage, but it is very difficult to rush out of it. You can choose to go into marriage with your eyes closed, but I doubt if you can remain in it without opening your eyes. God had a purpose, a design and a plan when He said:

It is not good that the man should be alone; I will make him an help meet for him.

How did God create Eve, Adam's wife?

And the Lord God caused a deep sleep to fall upon Adam, and he slept: and he took one of his ribs, and closed up the flesh instead

Deliverance From Spirit Husband and Spirit Wife

thereof; And the rib, which the Lord God had taken from man, made he a woman, and brought her unto the man. And Adam said, This is now bone of my bones, and flesh of my flesh: she shall be called Woman, because she was taken out of Man (Genesis 2:21-23).

The passage above gives us a very important revelation. Marriage is not based on human imagination. God the architect, the builder and the sustainer of the home, had a divine blueprint for every marriage. He brings two people together in marriage for a purpose.

God is meticulous even when it comes to the issue of marriage. He brings two people together with mathematical precision. He knows the man or woman who will make you fulfil His divine purpose for your life. If you are a sister, somebody's rib was used to create you.

If you are a brother, your rib was used to create a sister, once God has ordained that you will get married. The crucial question then is how do I get to know my God - appointed partner? This is a question that you must answer. Your success in life depends on it.

The truth is that your destiny in life is attached to your partner. Your divine helper is your partner.

Marriage is stronger than family tie. The consequences of getting married to the wrong person can hardly be enumerated. It is tragic to pick the wrong rib. Once you get married to the wrong person your destiny is affected. The devil is very intelligent. He knows the potentials that are inherent in a successful marriage. This explains why he hates any marriage that is capable of causing havoc to his kingdom.

That is why he is the number one enemy of your marriage. He fights tooth and nail to destroy it.

Why are many marriages breaking down? Why are many couples contemplating divorce? Why are many believers finding it difficult to successfully pursue their programme in the area of marriage? The only answer to these questions is that the foundation has been destroyed. If you desire a good home you must take care of the foundation. Now is the time to look into the foundation of your marriage. A good start will result in a good finish. The moment the foundation is solid, the building will stand the test of time. A home that is built on the solid rock will stand.

I had an experience when I was studying for my doctoral degree in England that I would ever live to remember. A Nigerian acquaintance requested that I should accompany him to Gatwick Airport. I was somewhat curious and I asked to know what we were going to do there. He brightened up and said, "You are accompanying me to the airport because I want you to join me in welcoming my wife to England." I accepted to go with him since I wanted to share in his joy. The airport was unusually busy that day.

The fact that people were running back and forth signalled the arrival of a Nigerian Airways plane. The airport personnel as well as security agents were all on the alert. Those who boarded the aircraft began to alight one after the other. I expected my friend to locate his wife with ease but it surprised me when he brought out a photograph from his pocket trying to compare the face on it with the faces of some ladies who were arriving from Nigeria.

A lot of questions ran through my mind. After waiting for about 30 minutes, I could no longer keep quiet. I said to my friend: "I am sorry if this question will bother you. Do you mean you have never met your wife? Have you lost the memory of how she looks? Why have you continued to look at this photograph?" My friend smiled and came up with a shocking reply. "Let me confide in you, I have never met her before. This photograph was posted from Nigeria. I am supposed to get married to her because my parents arranged it."

We waited for a long time. It was like waiting for eternity. Just when I thought the posted wife would not arrive, a light complexioned lady sauntered towards our direction. My friend looked at his photograph again, stole a glance at the direction of the lady and called a name that elicited a response from the unknown lady, "Yes I am the one. Are you the man I am supposed to get married to?" That was how my friend's wife was posted to England. Unfortunately, the marriage never worked. Two years later, my friend's wife absconded with a German. What went wrong with that type of marriage? It was built on a wrong foundation. I have learnt to examine the foundation whenever I come across cases that border on marital distress.

What is your basis for choosing a partner? Are you basing your choice on beauty, financial ability and academic qualification? That kind of foundation will not support a building that you intend to live in for a lifetime. If you fail to make God the foundation of your marriage, you will regret your action.

Every instance of marital distress can be traced to a bad foundation. When you are planning to get married, you have to take a spiritual searchlight and examine the foundation. .

CAUSES OF MARITAL DISTRESS

The following are the causes of marital distress.

Marriage relationships that were contracted when you were strangers to God. Those who started their marriage without consulting with God will experience marital distress. The way you handle your marriage can be likened to the way a computer is utilised. If you put garbage into your computer system what you get out of it is a well-packaged garbage. A bad foundation will give you a bad building, no matter the amount of money expended on it.

Any relationship that is contracted or initiated when you are an enemy of God will fail. If a lady decides to hold on to a man who she met when she was in the world, she will build her marriage on the foundation of failure. Those who are partially born again will automatically go for a relationship that has no God in it.

A man who decides to marry a lady who has no relationship with God is storing up disaster for the future. If you get married to a godless man because of peer or family pressure, you will reap a bounty harvest of marital failure. If you join your hands with a child of the devil, that kind of marriage will not last, it will get into distress almost immediately you start it.

1 have stated time and again that besides hell fire, nothing is as bad as marital distress. The consequences of leaving God out of the choice of a partner far outweigh what you think you stand to gain. You can hardly afford to pay the price of self management in the area of marriage.

Holding on to your own choice and disregarding God's choice is likened to walking into the jaws of a hungry lion. The catastrophic consequences can never be imagined. you will live to regret it. It is an expressway into trouble, confusion and total failure.   Distress is inevitable;   The Bible states unequivocally that there is no fellowship or communion between light and darkness, they are diametrically opposed to each other.

There is no communion between the temple of God and the temple of idol.   There is no meeting point between children of light and children of darkness. Even if you choose to dine with the devil by cleverly using a long spoon you will end up being a loser. By the time you empty the content of the long spoon into your system, it poisons your entire system. I pity men and women who choose to operate a 'buy now, pay later' system. Such people regret every step taken outside God's will.

1 pity the smart Alecs of this world who think they can eat their cake and have it. They have always ended up biting their fingers. You can join the bandwagon, but you will never get

away from suffering the consequences. You can operate your life the way you like, but you must also get ready to pay the price. What you sow is what you reap. A farmer who planted nothing and went about telling his friends that he has an hectare of apples will become ashamed when he has nothing to show them during harvest. His story can be believed only for a short time and whoever tells it eventually bears the shame of self-deceits.

God expects you to burn the bridges that link you with the world immediately you decide for Him. Your value, plans and prospects will be swallowed by God's perfect will. You must burn the bridges that are capable of taking you back to the world. Your employer may threaten to give you a sack but you must consider the fact that it is easier to face the wrath of man than to face God's own wrath. It is better to lose a job than to lose the opportunity of getting to heaven.

Why must you succumb to the pressures of a man who keeps his own family intact and wants to ruin your future. I know of rich men who send their children to school in chauffeur driven cars and lavish care and comfort on them while they are ready to destroy the lives of other children. Beware! You must break every relationship that is capable of constructing and establishing a bad foundation for your marriage. Burn the bridges, disregard the promises and return the presents given to you by those who are likely to lead you to the dungeon of separation from the Almighty.

Marriages based on accidental pregnancy - Many people are married today not because they planned it that way, but because they were forced into it through accidental pregnancy. Such marriages are not based on love; they are born out of circumstances. That kind of marriage can best be (escribed as fire brigade arrangement. I do not know if you have ever watched fire brigade personnel in action. They are always in a hurry, they have no room for decorum.

A lady suddenly gets pregnant and everybody begins to panic. The parents of the two partners agree that the marriage be contracted to avoid the shame of accidental pregnancy. Whenever some parents discover that their daughter has been put in the family way, they forcefully instruct the man responsible for the pregnancy to marry the pregnant girl.

Marriages that emanate from accidental pregnancies are based on lust rather than love. True love will not put the other partner into trouble. Lust is careless but love is considerate. The people of the world often say, 'love is blind.' They are wrong. Perhaps what they meant to say is 'lust is blind'. Yes, lust is blind; it is also deaf and dumb. Lust makes people insensitive to others' well-being.

Sex before marriage - This leads to marital distress. Any sex outside marriage amounts to the construction of a satanic coffin. If you decide to construct a coffin for your marriage, you may end up being buried in it. The problem of premarital sex has become the order of the day. People now say if you cannot beat them, join them.

The situation is so alarming that teenage girls find it difficult to maintain chastity. Girls who are in their early teens are so morally loose that they have constituted painful embarrassment to their parents. By the time such girls gain admission to the university, they graduate into glorified academic prostitutes. That is how most lives have been destroyed. A lot of atrocities take place in the university campuses and have left many people bewildered and confused.

A particular incident took place in 1995. Members of our prayer warrior team were observing a prayer vigil while a strange appearance of five strange birds caught their attention. They sensed that the birds were not ordinary ones and they decided to issue judgmental curses against them. One of the birds landed on the ground, within the church premises, and transformed into an old woman. The members of the prayer warrior were surprised, but they knew that it was their fiery prayer that brought down the flying image.

This is no fantasy. I actually spoke with the woman eyeball to eyeball. She told me she came from a town located in the western area of Nigeria. According to her, she took off in the company of other powerful witches, to carry out an assignment at the University of Lagos. She made me to know that their responsibility was to strengthen cult activities in the University. She said, "Man of God, we have no business whatsoever with your church. In fact, it is a no-go-area for our class of witches. The only problem is that your church is located very close to the University campus. To get to our place of assignment we have to pass through the precinct of your church. We did not know that your men were holding a prayer meeting."

1 challenged her to give her life to Christ but she remained adamant saying. "It is impossible. I cannot. 1 have already sold my soul to the devil." Then she looked straight at me and said, "We know you. Your father died last year." I told her she was correct, I asked her to tell me how she knew that I lost my father. She reeled into a terrible laughter and said, 'You are asking me how I got to know that you lost your father? We operate a very powerful network and we have our agents everywhere."

Can you imagine that an illiterate witch, was given the assignment of supervising a university campus? The devil is really wicked. You can imagine what will happen to the university ladies who sleep with men at random as well as male students in the University, who are in the occult. Your guess is as good as mine.

Female university students operate under a terrible licentious spirit. How can you explain the case of a boy of 18 who goes about with dangerous weapons with which he harms innocent students? How can a young boy hack a fellow student to death with an axe? Such students are operating under terrible satanic influence. What that old hag disclosed to me made me to pity young men and women in the universities.

It pays to obey God. When the Bible says thou shalt not do so and so. such a commandment is for your utmost good. To get involved with premarital sex is to put your marriage into trouble. If you violate the word of God, your life will be invaded by terrible demons from the bottomless pit. You may choose to commit immorality and your pastor may never know it, but the devil will surely know you have violated a spiritual principle and he will afflict you. You are waging war against yourself and digging your own grave. if you are 25 or 30 years old and about five men are sleeping with you, you need serious deliverance.

Marriages contracted after demonic consultation - It is common knowledge that many African parents visit soothsayers or diviners to find out what the future holds for their children.

Whenever some believers inform their parents that they have been led of the Lord to choose their partners, the parents would quickly ask them to give them the names of such would-be husbands or wives. What do they generally do with such names? They go to the house of local witch doctors to ask them to check up the names with their gods. That is how many people's names have gone to demonic archives through consultation with fetish priests.

If you are very vigilant, you would have realized that African parents are fond of collecting the names of people they see around their children. If your marriage takes place after such a demonic consultation, it will end up in failure. Satan, being very clever, would use the information against your life, which will be the beginning of your marital failure. Whenever the soothsayer tries to consult with a higher demon, the devil will manipulate and seal your doom.

Satanic agents will not rest until they have succeeded in luring you into an unprofitable union. Even if the person's name you have given to your parents was capable of leading you into confusion and marital failure, such a fellow is likely to pretend and dance to your tune until he has succeeded in destroying you. If you are a lady, such a man will decide to 'accept' to join you in your church, and he would be regular until he has succeeded in taking you to the altar. You may experience the greatest shock of your life when he takes you home after the wedding and you come across occultic materials in the man's bedroom. He is likely to say, 'You can go to blazes. You are already married to me and there is no going back.' That is how the problem begins right from the first day.

How can the devil succeed in capturing such a lady? The devil knows that he can destroy people's destiny through leading them into destructive marital relationships. His intention is to lead as many young men and women to get married to their enemies. This is a very serious matter. You cannot afford to gloss over an issue as weighty as this.

I want you to close your eyes as you take this prayer point:

I shall not marry my enemy, in the name of Jesus.

Failure to address this issue may sentence you to perpetual suffering and regret. Even if you have never experienced what it means to suffer the consequences of bad marriage, you may have witnessed the travail of relatives and parents who are bruised by the jagged saw of marital failure.

Perhaps you can recall how your own mother suffered at the hands of your father. Perhaps you can also recall how another relative of yours was battered for life after receiving deadly blows from the hands of the monster called marital distress. Would you like to step into the shoes of those people? Of course not.

Many women who started their marital life on a wrong note have lived to tell stories of misery and woe. For example, although they suffered together with their husbands, yet they hardly live to enjoy the fruits of their labour.

If you do not want to have such bitter experiences, you must spend quality time to pay attention to your foundation. Prevention, they say, is better than a cure. Even if you eventually procured solution to your problems, the time spent as well as the scars from the wound will remain unforgettable.

Marriages enforced by ignorant parents - Some parents are fond of forcing their children into injurious marital relationships. Some parents are too anxious to see their children married, thus they coerce them into marriage.

If your parents force you into a relationship, whatever you suffer will be borne by you. You will not be able to blame them, but even if you do, it will not change your situation.

If a lady is seen with two or three men, who appear well off, the parents will likely have preference for a particular man. Your mother may say to you, "Who is this new man who has started visiting you? I do not want to see him. I want you to get married to that young medical doctor, who visited here a few months ago. That is my stand." The lady may reply saying, 'Mummy I cannot marry that medical doctor. He is not my kind of person. He is a womaniser. With that kind of man one cannot experience marital stability." The mother would persuade her saying: 'That is not a problem. It is very easy to tame a womaniser. Just satisfy him and give him good food and he will never go out again."

With that kind of statement, the mother may persuade her. If the lady succumbs to the pressure, she would eventually experience marital distress. No matter what she does, the man would continue to womanise. Of course, her mother will not be there each time the man comes home after a late night escapade. She can blame her mother but she would know that she is the one who suffers not her mother.

Some parents ignorantly commit their children to get married to someone from the same town or village regardless of what happens in the future. Such parents bring negative influence to bear on their children, because they feel that if their children marry from the same community such marriages are likely to stand.

What do you do if everyone from your village or community is a drunkard, occult practitioner, chieftaincy title holder, member of the white garment (fringe) church, member of the Jehovah's Witness sect or a nominal church goer? Must you get married to someone from your community? If you build your marital life on the foundation of ignorant parents, you

Deliverance From Spirit Husband and Spirit Wife

will regret your action.

Sexual pollution during your youth - In this environment many young people are sexually assaulted or lured into immorality when they are very young. Such an ugly experience leads young men and women into sexual promiscuity. Unless such victims go through deliverance, their traumatic experience will affect their marital lives.

If an armed robber rapes a lady, she is likely to suffer marital breakdowns. After such a lady has seen a medical doctor, she must also consult Dr. Jesus for spiritual sanitation and deliverance. Such a lady's life must be rid of all the evil things which the armed robber has transferred into her through sex. It is possible that some wicked spirits are bent on destroying your marital life.

Marriages in which blood covenants were formed - Many young people go into blind covenants to prove their loyalty to their partners. Some young men and women foolishly cut themselves with razor blades and formed terrible blood covenants without knowing the implication of what they were doing. Such covenants will work against your marriage.

Why should two young people who are yet to get married enter into any kind of covenant? If you say, "I am going to get married to you, if I disappoint you, let my days be filled with darkness and sorrow", you have formed a covenant. If you break it, you will come under a curse. Such people must go through deliverance if they want to experience freedom from evil covenants and curses.

Deliverance From Spirit Husband and Spirit Wife

Marriage established on the principles of "it is better than nothing" - A common saying goes thus, "Half of a loaf of bread is better than none at all." Really? That sounds like a demonic philosophy. If you go for a half loaf of bread in your marriage, you are going to live with it.

Will you opt for a marital relationship which you are going to manage when it is possible to receive God's best? Such a marriage will collapse like a pack of cards.

Marriages based on trial and error - Some people are ready to say yes to any man or woman they come across, perhaps because they believe they have waited for too long. Such people normally come up with statements like, "I am ready to say yes to any man who comes to ask my hand in marriage." Anything goes. If I keep on waiting for Mr. Right, I might end up waiting for forever. Let me try the relationship, who knows, it might work."

Such a trial and error approach will surely end up in failure. God never intended for us to approach marriage in a hit or miss way. God is the only genuine match-maker. He is the only manufacturer who can never make a mistake.

Marriages based on physical attraction - Physical attraction cannot sustain marriage. Beauty fades and appearance cannot give you lasting satisfaction. If your marriage is based on physical attraction, it will fail when your spouse begins to age. The beauty you saw yesterday may not be there tomorrow.

Some ladies go about saying, "I am still looking for my kind of man. I will get married to a tall, handsome man. If a man is not presentable, I cannot marry him." You can go ahead and marry Mr. Universe or Miss World, but you will discover sooner or later that beauty fades. Physical attraction will not survive when you face the nitty-gritty of marriage.

Marriages based on material interest - If your choice of a partner is based on material interest, your marriage will not last. It is good to live a comfortable life, but prosperity and material comfort cannot sustain a home. I know many millionaires who are divorcees.

I pity ladies who go about telling everybody: "The man of my dream must be wealthy. He must have at least two cars, six digit bank accounts, and must not be a tenant. My man must also be able to afford occasional overseas trips. I can never marry a poor man. I am not going to suffer in the house of any man." Such a condition will lead you into a terrible mistake. There are lots of young men who are quick to go for ladies who are comfortable and have a car. Immediately they sight a sister who owns a car, they begin to pray. Within a short time they come up with a vision. There are careless brothers who go to car parks to choose their wives. They ask the ushers and security personnel to give them names of single rich sisters.

Once they are through with their enquiry, they run to the marriage committee with such names. Unfortunately, such sisters are too busy to pray, they might say yes without finding out the will of God. Such ladies, who have waited for several years, generally grab whoever comes to them. It is after the

Deliverance From Spirit Husband and Spirit Wife

marriage has been contracted that the man realises that he has walked into a cage. If anything happens to the lady's fortune or wealth, the boat of their marriage will capsize.

Marriages based on satanic prophecies - When we talk of satanic prophecy people are likely to think about visiting a voodoo priest. Respected or popular prophets in white garment churches dish out satanic prophecies. It is unfortunate that some people who are married today were led by the nose, through satanic prophecies.

Some people attend churches where some so-called prophets and prophetesses spoke saying, "Thus said the Lord . . . You are going to come across your wife beside a tree around noon tomorrow. Just walk up to her, she is your God's appointed wife." Such a man will be confused as he would not know how to locate the appropriate tree, that is exactly how many a man has picked a deadly bomb for a wife.

Marriages established by donation of a spouse at a young age - It is the practice in some African countries that parents give out their daughters at the ages of eight, nine or ten to some wealthy businessmen or traditional rulers. The young girls grow up in the houses of their husbands. That kind of foundation will lead to marital failure. How can a young girl of 13 or 15 cope with marriage? She will end up going through the travail of marriage when she is supposed to be under the care of her parents. Such a marriage never works.

Marriages based on polygamy - Most African marriages in the past were polygamous. We thank God for the wonderful

68

changes which the Gospel has brought to our society. Polygamy is not the will of God and will never work.

A lady may go into a polygamous marriage just because she is pressured into it. After a year or two, she is likely to begin to seek for ways of coming out of it. There are some ladies who decide to get married to rich men who already have two or three wives. Such ladies will discover sooner or later that money cannot provide satisfaction.

Perhaps you come from a polygamous family, and you can remember what you have gone through. The problems often extend into the third or fourth generation.

Having examined these faulty foundations, you can now understand why many families are distressed. A bad foundation will not sustain any marriage. Even if the marriage ceremony was conducted in Europe or America it would not stand.

The success of your marriage is directly proportional to the strength of the foundation of your marriage. Salvation is the beginning of a successful marriage. The day you become a child of God, your life is taken away from a bad foundation and placed on Jesus the solid Rock, and with Him your marriage will never fail.

The Bible says,

If the foundation be destroyed, what can the righteous do.

The righteous can only rely upon what is written in Jeremiah 32: 17:

Ah Lord GOD! Behold, thou hast made the heaven and the earth by thy great power and stretched out arm, and there is nothing too hard for thee.

It is possible that your foundation was really bad, but you do not have to worry. God can change your foundation. He will bring such a fantastic transformation into your situation that you will be pleasantly surprised.

Some ladies come to narrate their peculiar experiences saying, "Man of God, I do not understand what has been happening to me. Men used to pester me before I was born again. But since I gave my life to Christ no single man has spoken with me. Tell me what is wrong with me?" Such people need not worry. That kind of situation is an indication of the fact that the devil had terrible plans for their lives before they knew the Lord. The devil is now terribly angry now that they have escaped from his kingdom. The devil will continue his attempt to prevent your divinely-ordained partner from receiving divine revelation.

STEPS TO BE TAKEN BY THE RIGHTEOUS

Identify your 'foundation' - You must ask yourself the following questions.

- What kind of foundation or background do I have?

- Have I identified all the problems that are capable of affecting my marriage?

- Have I recognised what my parents did deliberately or ignorantly to affect my marriage?

- Am I under any yoke, curse or bondage?

- Am I trying to build my marriage along the lines of marital distress?
- Have I covered anything which is capable of affecting my marriage?
- Am I deliberately building my marriage on a bad foundation?
- Have I sowed any bad seed that is capable of destroying my marriage?

You must provide answers to these questions. You cannot make any progress until you have identified your foundation. You must spend quality time on this important step. You must be ready to deal with all avenues for a satanic incursion into your marriage.

Confession of sin and repentance - You must confess your sins and repent wholeheartedly. Repentance will earn you a transfer from the platform of bad foundation to the mountain-top of victory and success in marriage. Confess your sins and tell God you will never go back to them.

If you conceal or hide your sins, the devil will continue to use them as a legal weapon for leading you into marital destruction. Repent today and you will experience a turn around in your marriage.

Aggressive and well-targeted prayer - You can only build your life on a solid foundation by employing aggressive and well-targeted prayer. The devil is so wicked, he is not ready to allow you experience a successful marital life. He will not yield unless he is subjected to repeated prayer bombardments.

Many ladies and men will never get married unless they are ready to pray fervently. The devil knows that if he allows you to have things easy in the area of marriage, he would lose the battle. That is why many people have fought their toughest battles in the area of marriage.

A lot of people will have to employ the weapon of dry fast, aggressive warfare prayer, vigils and serious prayers of agreement before the devil will shift his ground.

Breaking of evil covenants - Your marriage can only be successful, fruitful, progressive and trouble-free if you are ready to break evil covenants. If you go into marriage while evil covenants are still in place, that marriage will not succeed. Such a marriage is a miniature hell on earth. You must break every yoke and release yourself from bondage.

Breaking of curses - No man or woman should ever go into marriage when personal or ancestral curses are still operating in his or her life. A curse will cancel all the goodness which God has programmed for your marriage. You must go through deliverance to get all curses in your life broken before you go into marriage.

Restitution - I have stated time and again that the devil is a legal expert. He is also the accuser of the brethren. If you fail to do your restitution the devil will have a case against you in the demonic kingdom. The moment you do your restitution, you become free completely.

Intercession - You can clear a lot of debris from your

Deliverance From Spirit Husband and Spirit

foundation through intercessory prayer. Prayer is the greatest pill that can grant you immunity from marital sicknesses. Intercession will also affect your partner and prepare him or her for a future marriage.

Finally you have to take steps to clear satanic pollution from your marriages. You need to allow the divine axe to go right down to the root of your marriage and uproot unprofitable plantations. You need to pray for the deliverance of your marriage from the polluting influences of anti-marriage forces. You need to paralyse and dismantle every evil pipe releasing pollutants from the foundation of your marriage. You need to invite God of the new beginnings into your home.

To end this chapter, pray this prayer point with fire in your voice.

Spirit wife I spirit husband, release me, in the name of Jesus.

CHAPTER FOUR

Dealing With Spiritual Armed Robbers 1

The subject under consideration, in this chapter, is one that is capable of translating you from the valley to the mountain-top.

This is a unique topic which will take you into new thresholds of spiritual warfare. To benefit maximally from this message you have to imagine that you are seated right now in the school of deliverance. You will learn new lessons, practise new ideals in spiritual warfare, take unusual steps and say prayer points which may sound rather strange.

If you ever attended a deliverance session, you would have realised that anything can happen during the session. You must therefore expect the unexpected. Open your heart to receive the spectacular and get ready for the unprecedented. We are going to experience deliverance, freedom, unusual power encounters, victory and dominion over wicked

Deliverance From Spirit Husband and Spirit Wife

stubborn spirits and the demonstration of the victory that is our bonafide possession in Christ.

I can assure you by the spirit of God that you will not remain the same after participating in this school of deliverance. Jesus is the great deliverer; the Holy Ghost is the great teacher and the deliverance minister. Open your heart to God so that you can receive your full deliverance.

There are certain situations in life which cannot be solved by employing ordinary methods. I have counselled and prayed for many men and women who got to a point where they became confused, just because they did not know what to do to solve life's problems, most of them battled with their problems for 20 or 30 years. Some even wished themselves dead because they were tired of being mutilated and bruised by the jagged saw of stubborn problems.

Some considered calling it quits with Christianity. They wanted to consult powers which reside in the devil's domain. They were ready to take wrong steps because they were at their wit's end, spiritually speaking. What shocked me is the fact that most of these people were members of Pentecostal churches and had been Christians for several years, yet they did not know how to cope with life's problems. Ignorance kept them in the dungeon for several years.

Another surprising fact is that the ease with which they received solutions to their problems was a very big surprise to them. They discovered that there was a world of difference between their former Christian orientation and their experiences in the school of deliverance.

God has granted us the wisdom to turn our services into schools of faith, deliverance and spiritual warfare. The practical session in our school of deliverance has produced outstanding testimonies. God has transformed paupers into millionaires, slaves into princes and princess, sickly men and women into robust and healthy men and women. These people, who were harassed by demons, became demon chasers. Those who were sentenced to non-achievement became exceptional achievers.

Those under the stubborn yoke of sin became holy men and women. Men and women who suffered hallucinations, mental disturbances, mind blindness, nightmares and attacks by masquerades and other strange experiences, became completely free. Each person has a success story, a testimony and experiences that border on the miraculous.

The story of what happens in our school of deliverance can hardly be told on this side of eternity.

I congratulate you that you are part of that school by the virtue of the fact that you are reading this book.

I wonder if you will be able to keep track of the multiple testimonies that God will bombard you with. Just open your heart, obey all the instructions and get ready for divine visitations. Your candidature in the school of deliverance will cause your history to be re-written

II Corinthians 11:14-15 introduces us to the most wicked masquerade in the world. We are brought face to face with the fact that no one can masquerade like the devil in the entire universe.

And no marvel; for Satan himself is transformed into an angel of light. Therefore it is no great thing if his ministers also be transformed as the ministers of righteousness; whose end shall be according to their works.

Satan is the most elusive masquerade. Shifting positions or changing into various costumes is his stock in trade. Why does Satan masquerade? It is to deceive and to be able to unleash havoc on men and women without any inhibition.

CATEGORIES OF ROBBERS

Some armed robbers operate internationally, others nationally, while the sphere of operations of some is the local environment. Some armed robbers use the most sophisticated guns available, while others use cutlasses, axes and knives. The timid pickpocket, whom we come across at the bus stops are also robbers. Bus conductors, who refuse to give you change when you pay them, are junior thieves in the school of robbery. The person who steals meat in the pot and cuts the other piece into two to make up the number, knowing that the pieces of meat were counted, is also a thief.

Some children operate as clever young thieves by sipping from their daddy's drinks and adding water to it to ensure that the drink is still at the same level. The man who carries a gun in broad daylight or under the cover of darkness is an expert in the school of banditry. Thieves in this category are called armed robbers. They are armed with dangerous weapons which they use to threaten their victims and rob them of their valuables and attempt to kill if they come across any resistance.

SPIRITUAL ARMED ROBBERS

Spiritual armed robbers do not look out for properties like video players, electronic music machines, television sets, computers, micro wave ovens, pressure cookers, food mixers, trinkets, money, cars and other expensive gadgets.

This category of armed robbers does not go after physical items. It is obsessed with the quest for spiritual items. Its goal is to invite, plunder and steal what is confined to the realm of marriage in the physical realm.

These armed robbers exploit two things; the mystery of marriage (sexual union) and the mystery of human appetite. They are bent on invading the realm of the mysteries of marriage.

- These spiritual armed robbers spend their time sponsoring physical and spiritual demotion.
- They are responsible for the downgrading of their victims.
- They disgrace the lives of their victims.
- They dismantle good things in the lives of their victims.
- They divert the destinies of their victims.
- They make their victims to become disillusioned, confused and tired of living.
- They sponsor defeat and discouragement.

Deliverance From Spirit Husband and Spirit Wife

- They lead their victims into the dungeon of diseases and demonic bondage.

They carry out these evil activities by exploiting the mystery of marriage and mankind's crave for appetite satiation.

IMPORTANT STATEMENTS

I want us to consider these important statements which are foundational and crucial to the understanding of this topic.

The two most powerful gates through which demonic possession is introduced into the lives of men and women are the mouth and the sexual organ. Evil spirits have continued to use these two gates as their best entry points into the lives of millions of people.

The most powerful drive, apart from the urge to remain alive is a sexual urge.

Physical virginity is different from spiritual virginity. These are two different issues.

Marriage is the only divine platform for sex.

In your own interest, do not go to bed with any man or woman with whom you are not married. If you violate this command, the act will open you up to an invasion from the demons and you may not survive it. The devil may deceive you by saying that you need that carnal enjoyment badly. He is looking for a way to roast you alive. If you allow five minutes enjoyment to paralyse your destiny, you are the most foolish person on earth.

Deliverance From Spirit Husband and Spirit Wife

Many people who are struggling to go through deliverance today are suffering the consequences of immorality failure. Many people who fail to exercise discipline or restraint over their sexual lives have lived to regret the moments of carelessness. They have continued to languish in misery, woe, poverty, sickness, spiritual attacks, shame, demotion and traumatic experiences.

It is very easy to yield to the dictates of your carnal nature but it is very painful to pay the price. You can spend three minutes going into an illegal sexual act and spend 20 or 30 years paying the price. You can commit immorality secretly but you cannot conceal its consequences.

If a man sleeps with a prostitute, the demons from the last seven men, who slept with the prostitute will invade his life. The consequences can hardly be imagined. These demons, with all their filth, will enter and destroy him. He will end up paying for trouble. That is how many people have been brought into bondage.

If you have ever slept with a prostitute, you have at least seven demons, if you have not gone through deliverance. If you have slept with a prostitute five times, you have probably collected 35 demons. Some people wonder if these things are real. I am sure you know that the devil is very clever. He is so crafty that he has made some demons so quiet and refined that they do not manifest violently. You could have up to 20 demons and still live like a gentleman. The demons will reside in you for several years without putting up any violent manifestation.

Deliverance From Spirit Husband and Spirit Wife

We have seen cases of some men who suddenly become mad without any previous trace of demonic possession. The devil is not stupid. He will continue to allow you to collect more demons until your cup is full. The moment you are filled up with demons, an explosion occurs sooner or later. The explosion can take place after you have passed the prime of life. It can also take place when you have got to the peak of your career.

Again, it can take place when you get married. The truth is that anything can happen. The devil will allow you to buy now and pay later, but you may end up paying with your life. How foolish it is for any man to miss eternity for a fleeting moment of carnal pleasure.

Many people wonder why they are so poor that they live from hand to mouth. Such people have forgotten that they are now paying for the free meal they ate from the devil's table.

Many people are wondering why their lives seem to be put on hold by the devil. They should realise that a single involvement with the devil is capable of leading them into perpetual bondage and servitude. You cannot eat your cake and have it. It you think that you are so smart that you can sow into the wind without reaping a whirl wind you are mistaken. The devil can deceive anyone who is ready to accept deceit. You cannot sow wild oats and reap edible seed. Wild seed will yield the same specie, no matter the amount of fertilizer that is applied by the farmer.

Deliverance From Spirit Husband and Spirit Wife

It is not only men who stand the risk of collecting demons from sexually lose women. If a lady sleeps with a man who has slept with a prostitute or one who is grossly immoral, the woman stands the risk of collecting demons from the last seven women whom the man slept with before sleeping with her. This is the strategy of the spiritual armed robbers whom we are considering in this chapter. That is why the Bible is clear on the consequences of committing immorality.

As already mentioned earlier, when you read about sex in the Bible, you will see that two descriptive terms are used to express legal and illegal sex. When the Bible says that a man "knew his wife", it is telling us that a man has a legal physical relationship with his wife. However, when the Bible tells you that a man lays with a woman it is giving you a picture of a man who is having an illegal affair or a sinful relationship with someone to whom he is not married.

Therefore, spinsters, bachelors and polygamous men are guilty of engaging in illegal sexual relationship with the opposite sex. Anyone who belongs to the company or those who are sexually loose opens himself up to a demonic invasion. To be involved with such a loose lifestyle is to make you a candidate of wicked spiritual attack.

A lot of people claim that they cannot do without immorality. Such people tell us, "I cannot do without having fun. It is part of my nature. After all, everybody is doing it" Such people will realise that the price to be paid for living in sin can hardly be imagined. They will continue to suffer the terrible consequences long after they finished their affairs. If

Deliverance From Spirit Husband and Spirit Wife

What I have stated so far has affected you, you need to make definite changes. The earlier you make those changes the better.

A lot of people are spiritually married without their knowledge. They have no idea, whatsoever, about the fact that they are into any form of spiritual marriage.

Children who are born out of wedlock are generally born with the spirit of fornication in their lives. If you have ever studied the lives of children that are born outside matrimony, you would have realised that they have in their spiritual genes some chromosomes of immorality. Such genes should be flushed out through deliverance. Many people are battling with serious sexual urges which they received from their ancestral lines.

The sexual urge in the life of men and women is so strong that it has become satan's prime target. A lady confessed recently concerning an evil assignment given to her by the devil to pull a man down. The man was someone who believed in leading a morally pure life. In fact, before he was captured, he had never had sex with a lady. The lady kept on trailing him until she succeeded in capturing him. Unfortunately, the fellow happened to be a man of God.

When the lady captured him, she ejected terrible spiritual poison into his body. He died instantly while committing immorality with the wicked satanic agent. The woman carried her bag and ran away. People discovered the man's corpse after the killer had gone. Nobody knew what happened. The lady made this confession after giving her life to Christ. Meanwhile, the life and the ministry of her victim had been destroyed and amputated.

I want you to close your eyes at this point as you take this . prayer point with spiritual violence.

My destiny shall not be amputated, in the name of Jesus.

Several men and women are completely ignorant of the assignment which satanic agents have carried out in their lives. Ignorance kills. The office executive who runs after his secretary is inviting spiritual bondage into his life. Some people are praying fiery prayers when they are already captured by *their* secretaries in the office. The devil knows that the easiest way to control the totality of people's lives is through the control of their sexuality.

Marriage was intended by God to take place in the physical realm. Any sort of spiritual marriage is an aberration, a gross violation of what God has ordained.

Many people are consciously or unconsciously married in the spiritual realm. A lot of people unconsciously feed from the table of the devil every day. Any food taken from the devil's table will give you spiritual cholera. This statement may not be easily understood by those who are not conversant with the school of spiritual warfare and deliverance.

I hope you have not forgotten that you are seated in a deliverance class as you continue to imbibe the revelation which you .are coming across. You will receive spiritual enlightenment that will ultimately grant you freedom from all kinds of known and unknown bondage.

You shall know the truth and the truth shall set you free. The more truth you know the more freedom you will experience.

There was a time when I did not know anything about deliverance and spiritual warfare. I was like any other man. However, God picked me up at a particular point in my life and gave me deep revelations which He mandated me to share with multitudes. Just like Paul the apostle, I choose not to be disobedient to the heavenly vision. God has therefore decided to reward obedience by granting me special favour and breakthroughs in the ministry.

The manner in which God has backed up what we are doing in the ministry shows the important place He accords the truth concerning spiritual warfare and deliverance in these end times.

I can recall what happened in my early days in the kingdom of God. In a dream someone found himself eating *gari* (a common dried cassava meal in West Africa) in a bucket of water. The meal was so unusually large that he had a very hard time taking it. By the time he managed to consume the large quantity of *gari*, he felt nauseated and constipated. Somebody gave him another bucket of *gari* in the same dream and forcefully told him to consume it.

By the time he woke up around 5.30 a.m., during the Islamic call to prayer, the taste of the local *gari* was still in his mouth. He rushed to his pastor to seek an explanation of his experience. His pastor did not help matters. "Did you have any meal before you slept," he asked? "No, I did not. I slept on an empty stomach," the brother replied. "Not to worry", the pastor said, "Your dream is a reflection of your state of mind."

Do you know what happened? The same pastor conducted the burial of the same brother, exactly one week later. The brother died because his pastor knew nothing about the reality of spiritual warfare. Ignorance is costly. It is possible that you have lost several things due to ignorance and spiritual folly. A lot of men and women have lost their lives because of ignorance, as far as spiritual warfare is concerned.

There is a spiritual mystery behind marriage. Sexual union goes beyond the physical realm. Sex is both spiritual and physical. Those who get involved with illegal sex are selling themselves into spiritual slavery. Let us read a passage which contains a revelation that is hidden from millions of people: "Know ye not that your bodies are the members of Christ? Shall I then take the members of Christ, and make them the members of a harlot? God forbid. What? Know ye not that he, which is joined unto the Lord, is one spirit. Flee fornication. Every sin that a man doeth is without the body; but he that committeth fornication sinneth against his own body" (I Corinthians 6:15-18).

I am sure you have read that passage before. Did you really understand what the passage is saying? Sex is a mystery. It unites the spirit, the soul and the body. Every sexual act is a covenant. A sexual covenant is much more powerful than many covenants. The only covenant that is as strong as a sexual covenant is the blood covenant. The Bible has not kept us in the dark as regards the mystery of sexual intimacy.

The passage that we read will open our eyes to the dangers inherent in committing immorality with a prostitute. Paul, the apostle said: "Shall I then take members of Christ, and make them the members of an harlot? God forbid!" It is a taboo for anybody who is a child of God to have sex with a prostitute. I do hope that there is no child of God, anywhere, who is reading this book who will open his eyes wide and go into immorality with a prostitute. Such a person is digging his own grave. Such an act will lead into destruction of destiny, "God forbid," said Paul the apostle. It should never happen.

That is the most dangerous and wicked thing that the devil can suggest to any one whom he wants to destroy.

It is often said, "Those whom the gods want to destroy they first make mad." May I say, he whom the devil wants to destroy he leads into the house of a prostitute, since he knows that it is the easiest and quickest way to destroy his destiny. Nobody can visit prostitutes and prosper. Men who visit prostitutes are always poor, sickly and prone to failure in life. Some men may say, " I cannot visit dirty prostitutes. I go for academic prostitutes." Such people are deceiving themselves. Prostitutes are the same, whether they operate from a hotel, a university campus, or in decent flats.

Prostitution is spiritual. Anyone who is involved with

harlotry or prostitution is a demonic agent even if such a fellow is a university graduate. Harlots and prostitutes belong to the same spiritual company but only to different categories. Often the idea of ladies selling their bodies for money on the campus is much more demonic than those who sell their womanhood in hotels.

Many men who were destined to be multi-millionaires have lost their destinies through sexual intercourse with prostitutes. A lot of people who are supposed to achieve great things in life have been re-assigned to useless functions in life. That is why the devil often leads those whom he hates most to commit immorality with prostitutes.

Most prostitutes are initiated into witchcraft, familiar spirits, occult societies and other demonic associations. The devil therefore, uses them to initiate multitudes. If you have sex with a prostitute, you become one body with the devil. Sex outside marriage is very dangerous. You may not have sex with a prostitute, but if you ever have sex with a lady who has committed immorality with someone who had sex with a prostitute you are in trouble.

Paul the apostle gave us the solution to the problems of sexual immorality by commanding us to flee from fornication. Many people are falling into fornication and adultery. To flee means to get away as fast as your legs can carry you.

If Samson had fled from every appearance of sin, Delilah would not have captured him. Many people blame the devil and satanic agents for luring them into sin when such people are simply disobedient. Immediately you know or sense that a particular thing comes as an appearance of sin, you are expected to flee from it.

Some Christian sisters are living in self-deceits. They lead hypocritical lives. They are so worldly in their dressing that their employers take them for glorified prostitutes. They wear indecent and tight fitting dresses knowing that they are revealing all the shapes of their bodies. They catwalk on high heeled or stiletto shoes as if they were participating in a beauty context. They wriggle their bodies and move as if they are trying to lure men into sin.

Such people comport themselves as if they are looking for men to commit fornication with. When a sinner senses the fact that you are looking for a sin partner he invites you saying: "Are you available?". "Don't tell me that rubbish. Don't you know that I am a child of God?" you might say. The man will continue to victimize you as long as you are not ready to cooperate with him: he may even sack you. You are to blame. The unbeliever did not see any trace of the glory of God in your life; your dressing and attitude portray you as a chronic sinner.

Sexual immorality is so delicate that the Bible commands you to run away from it. According to the revelation which is given to us through Apostle Paul, sexual sins affect the body and once the devil gets you, your body, spirit and soul will go into bondage.

Do not sin against your body. Sex is such a powerful

mystery that is capable of leading you into deep bondage.

It is indeed strange that some people find it difficult to break loose from their former sexual partners. The minds of so many people are still tied to their former boyfriends, girlfriends or sin partners. This explains why sleeping with women fragments or divides many people's lives into many disjointed parts.

Evil spirits know that marriage relationship is a very powerful covenant. They try to lead men and women into spiritual marriage relationship. Whenever they find it difficult to bring spiritual contamination into the lives of their victims, they resort to the use of a spiritual marriage to spoil the spiritual light of their victims. Having realised the fact that the spirit of man is the candle of the Lord they try to put out the spiritual candles of careless men and women through spiritual marriage. Once your candle is put out, you are bound to live the rest of your life in darkness.

Spiritual robbers are indeed wicked, spirit wives and spirit husbands are the most dangerous and wicked demonic agents in the spiritual realm. Some of these spiritual spouses operate as spiritual rapists. They forcefully rape their victims by coming to their victims in the dream to rape them. Spiritual wives and husbands are wicked armed robbers.

Let us briefly examine the different categories of these spiritual armed robbers.

Physical armed robbers. These spirit wives and husbands usually appear in physical forms. They attack their victims physically.

I know somebody who was physically abused by one of such spirits. The man told me that he was attacked by a physical spirit wife at exactly 4.00 a.m. every day. The man, who had these experiences before his conversion, was actually married. The spirit wife would enter his bedroom and force him into immorality, even when the man's wife was physically present. The strange thing was that the wife of the man was not able to see the spirit wife. The spirit wife would engage him in a wicked sexual orgy until it was time for the man to wake up in the morning. And the man went to work tired and sickly every day.

Many people have that kind of strange experience today.

Conscious and unconscious spiritual partners. Some wicked spiritual partners behave like the wind. Although the wind cannot be seen physically, nobody is in doubt when it is blowing. The effects of these spiritual partners are felt by the victims even when they cannot be seen.

Spiritual prostitutes. Some of these spiritual armed robbers operate like prostitutes. They flaunt their bodies before innocent men and women.

Wondering spirits. This category of spirit wives and spirit husbands wander from one person to another seeking whom to devour.

THE GOALS AND OBJECTIVES OF SPIRITUAL ARMED ROBBERS

What then are the goals and objectives of these spiritual armed robbers? What are the assignments given to them by the devil? The devil has given them the following responsibilities.

Demonic initiation. Whenever these armed robbers attack anybody, they initiate them into various demonic societies.

Destruction of good virtues. Spiritual armed robbers destroy the virtues of their victims.

Siphoning the power of God. Spiritual armed robbers hate to see people who possess the power of God. Hence, they locate the power of God in people's lives and siphon it away with their evil pipes.

Late marriages. Spiritual armed robbers who operate as spirit wives and spirit husbands are the brains behind late marriages in the lives of men and women.

Inability to get married. Some men and women find it difficult to get married even when they are 40 years and above. These men and women are suffering from the attack of spiritual armed robbers.

Family discord. A home where the husband and wife fight every day is under the attack of spiritual armed robbers. The misunderstanding, quarrelling, arguments and fighting partners are sponsored by spirit wives and spirit husbands.

Terrible misfortunes. Spirit husbands and wives are responsible for the terrible misfortunes which happen in the area of marriage. There are instances when a date for a Wedding ceremony has been fixed and the bridegroom suddenly develops a strange mental sickness. The man becomes mad and begins to talk rubbish. At other times the bride becomes involved in a terrible accident. Spirit wives and husbands are responsible for this kind of calamity.

There is the story of a man who woke up on his wedding day and began to fight everybody. He told everyone around him: "You can all go to blazes. I am no longer interested in the wedding ceremony." They asked him, "Why are you behaving this way? I am sure that you know that everything is ready. We have cooked delicious meals and we are expecting your in-laws." The man replied, "Don't speak rubbish to me. You better get away from here or I will shoot every one of you." The embarrassed family members began to run helter skelter in search of help. Spirit wives are responsible for that kind of strange development.

Other people who suffer this kind of fate make decision to get married one day and wake up the next day to say that they are not interested in getting married. They shift wedding dates from month to month until the, families of the bride and bridegroom are tired. The activities of spirit husbands and wives are getting multiplied every day.

Strange dreams. Spirit wives and husbands are responsible for all kinds of strange dreams. Their victims often see themselves getting pregnant and having children in the dream. Some of their victims have given birth to as many as ten children in their dream without having a single child in

93

real life.

Blockages of the progress of homes. Spirit wives and husbands consider the wife or the husband of their victim as rivals and therefore block their progress.

Giving birth to abnormal children. Many people give birth to abnormal children as a result of activities of wicked spiritual spouses. Many of us do not know that a lot of evil angels move from one place to another to contaminate human beings. Such angels are responsible for the conception of some babies. We have seen lots of abnormal babies in African societies.

A young girl was brought for prayer because she had both male and female reproductive organs. The Lord revealed to our ministers that the girl was conceived through interference by evil spirits. Such evil spirits are still active today.

Abnormal menstrual cycles. Many women suffer abnormal menstrual circles as a result of the attack of spirit husbands. Some women also suffer painful menstruation due to the attack of spirit husbands.

Miscarriages. A lot of women suffer miscarriages due to terrible attacks from the camp of wicked spirit husbands.

Inability to secure a partner. Many women and men find it difficult to secure a partner simply because they are married in the spiritual realm.

Lack of interest in marriage. A lot of people have no interest whatsoever in marriage because an evil spiritual marriage is subsisting. Some Christian sisters or brothers go about saying that they have no plan for marriages even when they have grown very old. How can somebody think of getting married in the physical realm when such a person is married in the spiritual realm? A spiritual marriage will always hinder physical marriage.

Prostitution. Prostitution is influenced and established by the powers behind the evil spiritual marriages. They set up a network of prostitution to capture more victims.

Breast cancer. This is one of the activities of spiritual armed robbers. The issue of breast cancer has become so bad in Europe that it is the most dreaded disease. Some ladies whose mothers died of breast cancer, go to the hospital to remove their breasts even when there is no single trace of the cancer of the breast in them. They resort to that step to avert the possible occurrence of breast cancer in them.

Strange sickness. People who complain that some strange unseen objects are moving all over their bodies are suffering from attacks from spirit husbands and wives. Those who complain that certain things are moving round their stomachs are also being attacked by spirit wives and husbands. Those who see blood in their dreams are also victims of spiritual spouses.

Family unrest and divorce. Wicked spirit husbands and wives occasion instances of family unrest and divorce.

Polygamous tendencies. Spirit husbands and wives are responsible for polygamous tendencies. They make it impossible for men and women to stay with one wife or one husband.

Prolonged pregnancy. Evil spiritual spouses attack their victims with prolonged pregnancies. They are anchorages of such abnormal occurrences.

Total collapse of their victim's finances. Whenever a spiritual marriage is in place, wicked spiritual spouses orchestrate and execute the collapse of the finances of their physical partners.

Regular sexual dreams. Spirit husbands and wives are responsible for sexual dreams. That is their major avenue for making physical contact with their victims possible.

Sexual thoughts. Spiritual spouses make their victims to go into sexual fantasies. The activities of these wicked spirits are so numerous that I want you to get ready to pray at this point. I want you to realise that the kind of the prayers to be prayed against these types of spirits are not gentle prayers. These spirits must be handled with iron fists since they are stubborn. Unless you bombard them mercilessly, they are not likely to burge. They do not easily release their victims until they are given a tough fight. Perhaps the spates of spiritual attacks and turbulence which you are going through in your home at this moment, may be due to the fact that you are spiritually married without your knowing anything about it.

A lot of women have wondered why they are childless after they had been married for several years. Their husbands had contracted spiritual marriages before getting married to them. Therefore, the spiritual wives have vowed to teach those women a lesson. Some men are suffering in their marital lives simply because they did not know that their wives had been married to spiritual husbands before they came together. That is why things are not going on well in the home. The spirit wives are angry with those men. They leave traces of their anger.

These spiritual rapists plant many of the strange sicknesses which people suffer in their bodies. They inject their poison into the body of their victims thereby polluting them. It is when such partners are polluted that doctors begin to say that their sperm count is too low. Such situations may be given medical explanation but they are offshoots of spiritual pollution.

I want you to close your eyes and raise your voice like thunder as you take the following prayer points.

You spirit husband/spirit wife, scatter, in the name of Jesus.

Evil marriage in the spirit, scatter in the name of Jesus.

You conscious or unconscious spirit wife/spirit husband, release me by fire, in the name of Jesus.

Recently, I got a letter from the United States of America that made me realise that the problem of spirit wives and spirit husbands are prevalent in all parts of the world. A concerned Christian woman, who was reflecting the mood of most American women, wrote the letter. Her letter made me to know that many foreign men and women need urgent help. Before I received her letter, I had taught that the

Deliverance From Spirit Husband and Spirit Wife

problem of spirit wives and husbands is only among Africans and third world peoples.

She wrote, "Dear Dr. Olukoya. Is there anything you can do to help those of us who live in the United States of America? We need urgent help because 80 per cent of the women here have spirit husbands but they do not know that it is a dangerous phenomenon. Can you come to the Christian Broadcasting Network, an American television station, to enlighten us so that women who are suffering can be rescued and set free before it is too late?" I kept her letter.

Another letter was written to me by an American minister very recently. I was shocked when I observed that his own complaint also bordered on the problem of evil spiritual spouses. He was asking for help because a witch had fired an arrow into his reproductive organ. The letter was not written by a black man. It came from a white American. The two letters made me know that Christians from the western world are beginning to become aware of the activities of spirit wives and spirit husbands.

Just as it happened in the sixth chapter of the book of Genesis, spirit beings are becoming sexually involved with men and women. The same evil spirits who practised what happened in the book of Genesis seem to have made our generation the season of unprecedented spiritual sexual attacks. Spirit beings have turned their focus on human beings to cause them serious havoc.

If you fail to trace the sources of your problem, you may

remain in that condition throughout your life. For example, if your poverty and lack of progress are occasioned by spirit husbands or wives, you may continue to live in abject poverty, if you fail to institute a divorce against the spiritual spouse.

A man, who is married to a demonic woman in the spiritual realm, will be rendered poor so that he will be prevented from gathering enough money to marry a wife physically. A man who has a spiritual wife would be prevented from enjoying peace in his physical marriage so that the spiritual wives will continue to exercise control or dominion over him.

THEIR WEAPONS

Finally, let us examine the weapons which are used to enslave victims of evil spiritual marriages. What are the hooks that spirit wives and husbands use to capture their victims?

Dresses, adornments and hair style that arouse the sexual interest of wicked spiritual spouses. I must tell you the truth: most the dresses which many so-called Christians wear are capable of attracting the attention of spirit wives and husbands.

Demonic hair styles, tight-fitting dresses and licentious appearances are capable of making spirit wives or husbands to seek demonic sexual relationship with you. The mistake which is often made by some Christian sisters is failure to recognise the facts that just as physical appearances, which are sponsored by carnality, are capable of attracting physical men, it is also capable of attracting wicked spirit

Deliverance From Spirit Husband and Spirit Wife

husbands. Many sisters do not know that many evil angels move around with wicked appetites for the daughters of men.

If you make yourself an object of temptation or attraction to wicked spirits, they will forcefully drag you into a demonic relationship.

if you ever desire freedom from spirit husbands, do not wear dresses that are meant for men. The so-called Christian ladies who put on trousers are trying to court evil spiritual husbands. Many Africans try to justify themselves by saying that many tongues-speaking American Christians wear trousers. Anybody can justify himself or herself. I have come across Bible women overseas. The Christian women who are members of the church which I attended when I was studying in England, dressed scripturally. I happened to be the only black man in that church. None of the ladies came to the church wearing slacks or trousers. I was surprised to see them cover their heads the way we do in Africa.

Sexual looseness and perversion. Sexual demons are very powerful. They can enter through the eye, through the ear, through participation and through transfer. They also transfer into people's lives through inheritance. Other entry points include masturbation, pornography, watching films which feature naked men, homosexuality, lesbianism, oral sex, bestiality, incest, rape, occult sex, fornication, adultery, prostitution, filthy thoughts and conversation, sexual flashbacks (committing sin with somebody in your mind), promiscuity, flirting, the lust of the eyes, the lust of the flesh and inordinate affection.

Deliverance From Spirit Husband and Spirit Wife

Our university campuses have become citadels of prostitution. Each time I go to a university campus to minister, I am always moved to tears. I always pity young university students who become loose immediately they become university students. They have allowed the devil to turn their so-called freedom from the clutches of their parents into instruments of bondage.

Sex outside marriage. This is one of the hooks, which the devil uses to lead men and women into bondage. Sex outside marriage will lead you into the clutches of spirit wives and spirit husbands.

Living in sexually polluted environment. Spirit wives and husbands are fond of using spiritually polluted environment as hooks for capturing many victims. Some people have ended up living in houses that were formally used as enclaves of prostitutes.

Unknown to such people, such houses were renovated and adapted to residential purposes. If you move into such a house, you will receive demonic visitors every night. The demons, which the prostitute released into the atmosphere, will begin to invade the lives and families of the tenants.

Cloth that is dedicated to the marine powers. The moment you put on clothes that are dedicated to marine powers you will instantly become victims of abuse from the hands of evil spiritual spouses.

Inherited family spirit husbands and wives. Some families have either a single spirit husband or a single spirit wife who automatically marries everyone in that family. The moment that marriage is in subsistence every member of that family, young or old, is married in the spiritual realm.

A pathetic case was brought to my attention when I was writing this book. The problems bordered on the travail of a particular family. There were seven girls or ladies in a family. The eldest was 45 years while the youngest was 26 years but none of these seven ladies was married. Only one actually got married, but the marriage hit the rocks. She was sitting in their living room, one day, when a strange fellow walked in and poured corrosive acid on her husband. The man died from the attack of the family spirit husband who, unknown to them, had been married to all the sisters in the family. That was why they all suffered.

Perhaps you are suffering the same fate. What you have to do is to deliver yourself first before seeking deliverance for the other members of the family. You can help other members of the family only after you have succeeded in setting yourself free.

Unfriendly friends. Unfriendly friends have lured many innocent souls into the clutches of spirit wives and spirit husbands. The closer you are to anyone who is going through the problem of an evil spiritual marriage the more you are likely to become a victim yourself. If your best friends are involved in evil spiritual marriages, you will also become involved sooner or later unless you possess the fire of God. If you move with unbelievers who are spiritually married, the same spirit might flow into your life.

Deliverance From Spirit Husband and Spirit Wife

There are many types of friends. There are fair weather friends, parasitic friends, hypocritical friends (dangerous friends who smile at you and say something else behind you). casual friends and soul-mate friends. Soul-mate friends are very intimate friends. If you have a soul mate as a friend, he is capable of passing spirit wives or husbands to you.

Consultation of prostitutes and concubines. The devil will always use consultation with prostitutes and concubines as a bait with which to hook careless men and women.

Male or female circumcision by satanic agents. Parents who unwittingly allow satanic agents to perform the rite of circumcision on their children are responsible for handing them over to spirit husbands and wives. Circumcision for both female and male is so prevalent in Africa. This has become satan's cheapest tool for leading men and women into bondage. The blood got from the genitals of the female and male babies is spiritually used to contract marriage with them. It is common in African societies for parents to employ the services of native doctors or local community surgeons to circumcise their children.

Some of these local circumcision experts often use snail shells to circumcise newborn babies. That is how snail spirits have been introduced into the lives of many men and women.

Blood covenant relationship with partners. Blood covenants with male or female friends have led multitudes into evil spiritual relationships. There are instances of men and women who wanted to demonstrate their faithfulness to each other by going into blood covenants. Such people cut themselves up and lick each other's blood and an evil marriage is instituted.

Capturing of male seeds and organs of the body by the marine world. Anyone who has been subjected to the capturing of parts of his or her body by marine spirits becomes a victim of spiritual marriage.

Sexual assault at young ages. There is hardly any girl in Africa who escapes being assaulted by men when she was growing up.

Playful marriage. Some people go about saying that they have married babies and toddlers for their own children as a joke. Such careless statements are recorded in the spiritual realm. Some mothers refer to their male children as their husbands. Such acts are actually innocent on the surface but nonetheless have spiritual implication.

Some people's spiritual wives are their mothers. That is a very dangerous relationship. The points mentioned above are some of the hooks which the devil uses in catching men and women and forcing them into spiritual marriages.

Covenant rings and jewelry. Some people have been led into spiritual sexual intercourse with spirit wives and husbands as a result of wearing rings that are covenanted to the devil.

Many people wear jewelry, which are demonised, without their knowledge. Men and women who wear bangles, bracelets, rings, neck chains, pendants and other types of jewelry go into evil spiritual marriages because the items were dedicated to some demonic powers.

I have prayed with several men and women who found it difficult to maintain any relationship or sustain their marriages because they used bewitched rings and ornamental metals. Somebody gave them some beautifully decorated rings with which they were initiated into an evil spiritual marriage. They ended up being covenanted into a spiritual marriage after wearing such rings. Jewelry may appear harmless on the surface but I want you to know that demonic powers have turned them into objects of subtle initiation.

Condom. Many shades and forms of condoms are being introduced into the market in this generation. Although these condoms may not appear harmful on the surface, yet they are instruments of leading people into evil spiritual marriages. Many of these condoms were dedicated to satan before they were introduced to the market.

Also, evil powers know that the easiest way to capture men and women is through sex. These demonic powers know that millions of people all over the world are using condoms. They have decided to pass condoms through some secret demonic dedication with an eye on capturing the users.

The devil is so clever in using physical things to lead innocent men and women into spiritual bondage. He employs that method because he knows that men and women take things for granted and hardly expect satan to capture them through indiscriminate use of condoms. Through this means many people have contracted evil marriages with wicked spirits.

Religious baths. Many African religious groups subject their adherents to regular ritual baths. They take such people to the river and give them spiritual baths to ward off evil luck, calamities and terrible problems.

A lot of people have gone into marriage with water spirits after such ritual baths. If somebody goes into the domain of water spirits to have baths, such a person should blame himself or herself for whatever happens afterwards. When a local religious prophet or prophetess takes you for a ritual bath to solve your problem he or she will end up handing you over to spiritual husbands or wives from the marine world.

Marine spirits have converted occasions of ritual baths into seasons of picking men and women as wives and husbands. A ritual bath is exactly what the name suggests. You go through a ritual, which turns out to be a marriage altar through which many marriages have been contracted. If you have ever gone through any form of ritual baths, you are already married to a marine spirit husband or wife. You can only become free when you undergo serious deliverance.

Alcohol and drugs that alter the mind. The act of indulging in alcohol and other drugs which alter the mind, will create opportunities for demons to lead you into an evil spiritual marriage.

Fondling with children's organs. Satanic agents who

fondle with organs of male or female children have led such innocent ones into evil spiritual marriages. That is how many children have been given out as spouses to wicked spiritual husbands and wives.

Parents should be wary of people who claim that they are playing with their children. A wicked satanic agent can pretend that he or she is playing with a little baby when such a person is initiating the baby into a demonic marriage.

Manipulation of underwear by wicked forces. Wicked satanic forces often steal people's underwear and take them to some demonic meetings with the purpose of using them as points of contact. Some underwear are never returned.

Agents of evil spiritual husbands and wives use people's underwear as instruments to lead them into evil marriages. Some strange satanic agents sometimes return the underwear stolen by them. The moment their victims put on the underwear, they are connected to the demonic realm.

Rape. It is unfortunate that many armed robbers, nowadays, assault their victims sexually. Crime, robbery and burglary have got into such a bizarre dimension that those who are attacked often witness the rape of their daughters or wives besides losing valuable property.

The use of local charms. Africans often use protective charms otherwise called 'local insurance' to keep armed robbers away, avert accidents and other mishaps. Some people think that charms can provide them immunity from attacks by wicked enemies. They think it is possible to

Deliverance From Spirit Husband and Spirit Wife

become invisible to witches and wizards by the use of charms. Others use charms to procure or attract good luck, make men or ladies to fall in love with them and to make them resistant to satanic arrows.

The use of charms is so prevalent in Africa that many young and old carry them wherever they go for protective purposes. When a baby is born, some parents hang some charms around its neck to prevent it from being snatched by the cold hands of death. Some parents give their children powerful charms to use in the school. They believe the charms have potentials for activating the brain of their children.

It is unfortunate that many Africans collect charms from witch doctors or fetish priests without knowing the origin or sources of such charms. The devil is very clever. He can promise you protection if that is the only means through which he can capture you. The devil is very good at bargaining. He can offer protection on the surface while leading you into bondage underneath. Satan can hand you a powerful charm while drawing you into an evil marriage at the same time. Of course, the charm will work, but it will also work against you by leading you into a marriage relationship which you do not bargain for.

Many Africans are so addicted to the use of charms that they defend themselves by saying that they are not using the charms to harm anybody, but to protect themselves. That may sound very reasonable, but satan is not foolish, he has no free gift. If you obtain anything from any of his agents, you must be prepared to give something precious to him in exchange for it.

Many Africans have gone into bondage as a result of the use of charms by their parents or ancestors. It is possible that your grandfather consulted a fetish priest, seeking protection. Such a demonic agent might have given him a powerful charm. It is also possible that he used the charm successfully. The only fact, which may be hidden to him, is that the use of that charm has led him, his children and grand children into spiritual bondage. That is why nine out of ten Africans would need to go through deliverance to enjoy their lives.

Today, many Christians are children of priests and priestesses of local idols. Many of us have no idea of what our grand fathers and grand mothers did when they were worshiping idols. Most of what they did to give us security and protection in life were also used by the devil to lead us into bondage. That is how many people found themselves inside terrible demonic pits.

Traditional dances. Traditional dances are part and parcel of the culture of most African and Asian communities. It is possible that you participated in traditional dances several years ago and you may think that the dances have no bearing with what you are going through today. Traditional dances may appear innocent on the surface but it is deeply connected with idol worship.

Ladies who participate in traditional dances are generally half naked. They wriggle their bodies in consonance with the rhythms of the drums, which are demonic. If you watch men

Deliverance From Spirit Husband and Spirit Wife

who perform traditional dances you will be amazed at the manner in which they twist themselves and take acrobatic steps, and you will have no doubt in your mind that they draw some demonic powers from the deities of their communities.

As men admire dance styles and the mesmerizing steps of traditional dancers, evil spirits also enjoy the dances. If a lady dances very well, she is sure to attract the attention of a demonic spirit. Spirit husbands or wives cash in on such occasions for capturing men and women.

Offsprings of prostitutes, concubines and incestuous relationships. If the mother of a person was involved in prostitution, polygamy or incest before giving birth to that person, that individual is automatically a victim of an evil sexual relationship.

The use of demonic protective means by concerned parents. A lot of things are done by parents to protect their children, in this age of sexual promiscuity. The moment some parents know that their teenage daughter has attained puberty age they go to local fetish priests to procure charms which are supposedly capable of preventing the young girl from becoming pregnant.

Many parents have paid for charms which eventually led their daughters into marriage with spirit husbands. Some parents who place charms on their daughters to prevent pregnancy have also realised that their daughters struggle for pregnancy as married women.

Some African parents have gone as far as giving some

charms to their daughters which would make it impossible for any boy or man to have sex with them. Some of those charms are so powerful that men who attempted to have sex with such charmed girls have somersaulted and died on the spot. People who use these types of charms are often married in the spirit realm. The points which I have enumerated so far are part of the methods used by demons and satanic agents to lead men and women into bondage.

You must take care of your foundation or background if you want to be free from the attack which are perpetrated daily by spiritual armed robbers. If you have gone through deliverance, you must also ensure that you continue to live a holy life. Unless you are holy 'within and without,' spiritual armed robbers will continue to attack you.

Furthermore, if you are a victim of wicked attacks from spiritual armed robbers, you need deliverance. You cannot enjoy your life without experiencing total freedom from all sorts of spiritual armed robbers.

BACK TO THE BIBLE

You must be properly married according to the dictates of the Scriptures if you want to be free from wicked spiritual robbers. The standard of the Bible concerning marriage is very clear; one man one wife. Although polygamy is very common in Africa and nations, the Bible is very loud and clear on the fact that God wants a man to be married to only one woman.

Those who decide to disobey the word of God by

Deliverance From Spirit Husband and Spirit Wife

continuing to live as second or third wives or by being husbands of two or three women will always attract the attention of spirit wives and husbands.

This is the hour of deliverance. You must take the prayer points listed below with every iota of energy in you. You will have to make yourself available for deliverance after the prayer sessions at the last chapter of this book.

Dealing With Spiritual Armed Robbers 2

From your reading so far, you would have learnt that a lot of people have lost valuable spiritual property to wicked spiritual armed robbers. You would have learnt also that spiritual armed robbers are very clever and carry out their demonic activities with unnatural skill and dexterity.

Next is the examination of biblical methods for victory over all categories of spiritual armed robbers.

May I instruct you, at the onset, to cover yourself with the blood of Jesus as a result of the depth of what you are going to read in the pages of this part of the book? You need to soak yourself in the blood of Jesus in order to acquire spiritual immunity from all attacks, reactions, and counter-attacks from the camp of the enemy.

However, let me assure you that your victory is sure, it is non-negotiable according to the passages below:

Deliverance From Spirit Husband and Spirit Wife

And the God of peace shall bruise Satan under your feet shortly. The grace of our Lord Jesus Christ be with you. Amen. (Rom. 16:20).

Behold, I give unto you power to tread on serpents and scorpions, and over all the power of the enemy: and nothing shall by any means hurt you (Luke 10:19).

You need to prepare yourself for the battle by taking these prayer points:

I cover myself with the blood of Jesus, in the mighty name of Jesus.

Every good thing that has been stolen from my life by spiritual armed robbers, I recover them by fire, in the name of Jesus.

Every serpentine robber, I bruise your head, in the name of Jesus.

O God, arise and scatter the weapons of spiritual armed robbers, in the name of Jesus.

Evil arrows fired into my life in my sleep, come out by fire, in the name of Jesus.

Unless you are armed to the teeth, spiritually speaking, you may not be able to overcome some categories of spiritual armed robbers. Some spiritual armed robbers operate just the way physical armed robbers do.

Spiritual armed robbers attack people in their moment of weakness and in their areas of vulnerability. Spiritual armed robbers operate cleverly with subtility. They have stolen goods worth billions of dollars. It is rather unfortunate that many people's virtues, spiritual gifts, anointing, and power have been stolen.

These robbers have stolen the spiritual properties, which their victims spent their lifetime gathering together. They use two subtle methods:

They attack their victims by coming against them as spirit wives and spirit husbands.

They transform themselves into evil night caterers who forcefully feed their victims with evil spiritual delicacies.

They employ these two methods simply because they have been fully briefed by their master, the devil. They are aware of the fact that the two most powerful gates through which demonic powers enter the life of man are the mouth gate and the sex gate. The mouth and the sexual organ have been used by the devil to lead multitudes into gruesome captivity.

I am aware that some people visit the church to learn our method of praying as a means of protecting themselves from satanic attack. Such people actually 'fire' prayers without being ready to do their restitutions. Such people will end up multiplying their bondage. It does not make any sense to pray fervent prayers while holding tenaciously to adulterous or polygamous relationships. A man is not supposed to have more than one wife, while a woman is not supposed to be the second, third or fourth wife. Spirit husbands or wives will wax stronger if you are not ready to do your restitution and live according to the teaching of the word of God.

Many people have remained in their bondage through disobedience to the word of God. Such people have lost precious material and spiritual things by continuing to lead lives that attract spirit husbands and wives. If you want to have victory, you must be ready to align your life with the word of God.

A man spent three days in a serious prayer programme. Everything went on smoothly while he fasted and prayed for three days. As soon as he ended the programme, he had an experience which brought him down from a very high spiritual level. As soon as he closed his eyes that night, a woman was already waiting for him to seduce him. The woman moved close to him in a dream and succeeded in luring him into sex.

When he woke up the next day, he became aware that he had lost every spiritual blessing which he received during his prayer programme. The man lost everything, which he accumulated during those days of self-denial, fasting, aggressive prayer and rigorous reading and confession of scriptures. Spiritual armed robbers stole all his precious spiritual benefits.

IN THE STREETS

It is unfortunate that spirit wives and husbands have been released into the streets by the devil. It is impossible to identify these spirit wives and husbands without having the spirit of discernment. Most of the ladies that dress elegantly in the streets are not human beings. Some careless men pick up such people thinking that they are human beings.

Deliverance From Spirit Husband and Spirit Wife

Recently, somebody shared an experience with me which lends credence to the facts that there are many strange ladies on our streets. Careless men who are looking for extra-marital means of enjoying themselves pick up these demonic creatures.

A very educated and wealthy man decided to seek sexual pleasure outside his home. He got into his car and drove to the streets looking for a free lady. Hardly had he driven far when he came across a demonic beauty queen. He slowed down, beckoned to her and asked her to come into his car. He made up his mind that he was ready to pay whatever the lady demanded.

However, the man became surprised when the lady broke her silence after a brief ride in the man's car: "Excuse me, Mister, you have to bring your car to a halt and I have to get out right now. This is bad business. You are not the one to whom I was sent. If you care to know what my assignment is, I will tell you. I am looking out for a particular man. He is the one to whom I was sent from the demonic kingdom. The man is billed to give me a lift, have sex with me after which he will die instantly. I must go for the man. My time is running out. You are just lucky. If you have had sex with me, today would have been your last day on earth I must go now."

The lady opened the door and dashed out. The man was so surprised that he broke out in cold sweats. He was transfixed to the spot. He could hardly believe what had just happened to him. He realised that there was a narrow line between the enjoyment he was looking for and untimely death. It took him ten minutes before he could recover from the shock. He vowed that he would never look for any form of enjoyment outside his matrimonial home. God spared him out of His fathomless mercy.

If God could open your eyes to see the evil traffic between the demonic world and the physical world, you will be extremely careful. Many spiritual beings have invaded our world. The number of spirit beings who put on human flesh is so staggering that God has chosen not to allow us to see them.

If God had opened your eyes, you would have seen that most of the ladies who parade themselves in the streets are hermaphrodites in the spiritual realm. What you see in the physical realm may attract you and you may not realise that all satan's apples have terrible worms. A single bite will send poison into your body.

Many people who are struggling to get out of their problems do not know that they are the ones who invited satan into their lives through careless actions. Many people are struggling to breathe an air of freedom as a result of the bondage which they stepped into several years ago when they were looking for pleasure. The problem is so pronounced that 90 percent of African women are trapped spiritually. You can hardly find an African woman who is not being pursued by a demonic spirit husband in her dream. Demonic wives also assault many African men on a regular basis.

Those who have been visited by spirit wives and husbands

have rationalised their abnormal experiences. Some have said that sexual dreams are normal. Science may have a name for it, but it is abnormal. It is an evidence of spiritual bondage.

The greatest type of bondage is one which the victim chooses to accept as normal. Those who are under bondage without being aware of the fact that the devil has imposed a spiritual jail term on them will remain under bondage perpetually.

I want you to close your eyes right now as you take this life-changing prayer point:

O Lord, purge my system by fire.

If you actually spent quality time on that prayer point, you should have experienced a spectacular visitation from God.

STEPS INTO DELIVERANCE

How then can we experience deliverance from all kinds of attacks from demonic armed robbers?

Identify the doorways into bondage. You cannot find the way out of bondage until you have found the way through which you went into it. You must ask yourself the following questions.

- How did demonic wives or husbands gain entrance into my life?

- Did they come in during times of my carelessness and sexual looseness?

- Did I attract them through disobedience to the word of

Deliverance From Spirit Husband and Spirit Wife

God?

• Why am I a victim of spiritual sexual abuse?

• What did spirit husbands or wives see in me?

You must answer these questions.

Total repentance. If you want to free yourself from the clutches of evil spiritual spouses, you must also repent wholeheartedly. Half-hearted repentance will not suffice. If you repent of a sin today and go back to the same sin tomorrow, you do not know what scriptural repentance is all about. You must be sincere with God. God expects you to hate sin.

You must be specific when it comes to repentance in the area of immorality. You must go to God with a contrite heart. Mention the names of all your sinful sexual partners and ask God for pardon. You must also ask for cleansing from evil contaminations you got into by having sex with all the people whose names you mentioned to God. If you are not able to remember all the names, simply go to the Lord with the names that you can remember.

Renounce, reject and return gifts received through sinful sexual relationships. You cannot experience total freedom if you continue to hold on to the gifts which you received from past sexual partners. The gifts will continue to be used by the devil as points of contact between you and the demonic world.

Some ladies still go about with headgear which they received as gifts from their former boy friends. A lot of people who claim that they have new life in Christ still go about using the relics of their old sinful lives. How many so-called Christian ladies are still holding on to shoes, wrist watches, radio sets, television sets, cars and other gadgets which they received from men with whom they went into immoral relationships? Many ladies will have to destroy, return or throw away such items if they want to be free from spirit husbands. It is better for you to throw such things away and have victory than to retain them and remain in bondage.

In any case, you can decide to hold on to such items and continue to encounter demonic visitations from spirit husbands.

Plead the blood of Jesus. You must plead the blood of Jesus if you want to free yourself from every kind of bondage to spirit wives or husbands. You must plead the atoning and the redemptive power in the blood of Jesus.

Renounce the spiritual marriage contract. You must take exactly the same step that is generally taken secularly to end a marriage relationship. When a lady is tired of a man, she seeks a divorce. You must do the same. Tell the spirit husband or wife that you want the contract terminated. Issue a bill of divorcement against the spiritual husband or wife. You can take your case to the court of God, appealing with the Scriptures.

You can base your appeal on the legal backing given by the following Scripture.

Jesus answered and said unto them, Ye do err, not knowing the scriptures, nor the power of God. For in the resurrection they neither

marry, nor are given in marriage, but are as the angels of God in heaven (Matt 22:29-30).

Know ye not, brethren, (for I speak to them that know the law,) how that the law hath dominion over a man as long as he liveth? For the woman which hath an husband is bound by the law to *her* husband so long as he liveth; but if the husband be dead, she is loosed from the law of *her* husband. So then if, while *her* husband liveth, she be married to another man, she shall be called an adulteress: but if her husband be dead, she is free from that law; so that she is no adulteress, though she be married to another man. Wherefore, my brethren, ye also are become dead to the law by the body of Christ; that ye should be married to another, *even* to him who is raised from the dead, that we should bring forth fruit unto God. (Rom. 7:1-4).

NIGHT CATERERS

The subject of armed robbers cannot be complete without a brief discussion of their second method of operation.

Besides leading their victim into bondage through sex, spiritual armed robbers also resort to the use of night caterers to capture men and woman. The problem of evil night caterers has continued to baffle men and women in Africa in particular and in the world in general.

The devil has raised up evil caterers who specialise in preparing poisonous meals with which they destroy the lives of men and women. More than 70 per cent of Africans find themselves eating food in the dream. Such has become an avenue for leading many people into bondage.

Anyone who consumes polluted food offered by satanic agents will experience one problem or the other. Anyone who is fed in the dream is being contaminated through the mouth gate. Those who attend demonic parties where food is distributed in real life will eventually find themselves in bondage. Those who attend strange birthday parties and consume food that is offered there will find themselves in spiritual cages.

Those who eat animals sacrificed for ritual or religious purposes will also go into bondage. All those that collect charms from fetish priests to swallow will find themselves in a spiritual cage, sooner or later.

If a fetish priest has ever rubbed your body with an egg and later asked you to swallow it, you have been captured spiritually. Whenever you swallow anything that is either demonic in nature or unclean, it will cause you serious trouble. The devil uses these methods to lead men and women into bondage through the mouth gate.

Anyone who eats regularly in the dream will never be able to retain the anointing and the power of God. They will suffer incurable diseases.

A lot of people, who have taken foods that are poisoned spiritually in the dream, have developed a stomach ulcer. Those who are fed in their dreams often manifest, anger and uncontrollable fits of temper.

The devil uses sex and what is consumed through the mouth to lead people into bondage. He uses these two outlets as weapons of capturing men and women. He knows that it is naturally difficult for man to control the dictates of these two drives.

EVIL CONSUMPTION

Consumption of foods polluted by wicked spirits causes problems.

This happens through:

Night feeding. This is to cause sicknesses and to weaken the spiritual life of a person (see our book on "Victory Over Satanic Dreams").

Demonic parties and distribution of foods. This is a demonic way of introducing into one's life what one would naturally have refused to take.

Birthday parties. This happens sometimes in schools. It is used to transfer virtues and shorten life or to initiate children.

Consumption of demonically-inspired animal sacrifices. This is having fellowship with demons by eating at their table.

Consumption of herbalist/witch-doctor's materials.

Rubbing eggs on the body by a satanic agent.

Drinking blood from a witch-doctor or as a covenant with another person.

Drinking concoctions presented by demonic people.

The children from polygamous homes can hardly be free from this local evil attack.

Feeding of the mother and babies with honey, oil or rat on naming ceremonies days.

Deliverance From Spirit Husband and Spirit Wife

Consumption of 'puff-puff' or bean-cake made in celebrating the '40th day' of the dead.

Consumption of 'puff-puff' (or bean-cake) made for demonic parties.

Drinking olive oil from demonic churches.

Drinking holy water from demonic churches.

This is what the Bible says on feeding from the table of the devil. 1 Cor. 10:21 says,

"Ye cannot drink the cup of the Lord, and the cup of devils: ye cannot be partakers of the Lord's table, and of the table of devils."

.Eating from the devil's table results in:

−Not feeling the touch of God or hearing from God.

−Sinning without being troubled.

−Constant negative visions.

−Spiritual weakness.

−Incurable diseases.

−Constant sickness.

−Depending on drugs.

−Unexplainable stomach ulcers.

−Things moving all over the body.

−Fierce anger or an uncontrollable temper.

The devil's food is very cheap and you do not have to be rich to afford it. The food may hide in your body and not manifest for years. It is a very popular evil arrow in our environment where people love free and cheap food.

Deliverance From Spirit Husband and Spirit Wife

Solution

1. Repentance.
2. Ask the Lord for spiritual purging. (Use our book "Pray Your Way To Breakthroughs" or prayers at the back of this book.)
3. Cancel the evil effects of every evil consumption.
4. You may need to go for deliverance if it is very serious.

OUR DEFENSIVE WEAPONS

Now that you are aware that the devil has concentrated his efforts on these two areas, you are likely to be interested in knowing how you can defeat the devil in these areas. A man or a woman who can conquer satan in these two areas will be victorious in every area of life.

If you have suffered attacks in the areas highlighted in this book, what kind of defensive weapon can you use to defeat the devil?

Regular self-examination. You must subject yourself to regular, self-examination if you must be free from demonic attacks. You must examine yourself to ensure that you are not living in sin in any area of your life. Sin will create avenues for afflictions and oppression. Sin will lead you into bondage.

If you allow anger, malice, gossip, backbiting, lying, lust and other hidden sins in your life, you will also experience spiritual bondage that is often hidden from the glare of the public.

Deliverance From Spirit Husband and Spirit Wife

Soak yourself in the word of God. The Bible says, "Let the word of Christ dwell richly in you" (Col. 3:16).

Bondage and spiritual attack in the lives of many people can be traced to the dearth of the word of God in their lives. The lives of many people are so shallow when it comes to the knowledge of Scriptures that demons find a comfortable house in them. The devil hates the word of God. The more you have the word of God in you, the more difficult it is for the devil to gain any in-road into it. Jesus conquered the devil through the word of God.

Spirit husbands and spirit wives will not come near you if they know that your life is completely soaked in the Scriptures. However, they will always attack you if they know that your heart is filled with the lyrics of worldly songs, local proverbs and useless words. Many Christians need to beef up the spiritual wall of the word of God in them to give them any meaningful spiritual covering.

We do not intend to turn believers into prayer point factories. Our goal is to prepare people for heaven. The only advantage is that our warfare prayers can lead heaven-bound saints into victory in all areas of their lives. The ultimate is heaven, not victory over witches in this world. If you attack the evil in your prayer without referring satan to the Scriptures, your prayer will not move him.

Praise and worship. Praise the Lord every day, especially before going to bed. Fill the last minutes before going to bed with praise worship, thanksgiving and expression of gratitude

l

to God.

The devil finds it difficult to attack someone who worships God and brings down His divine presence before going to bed.

Ask the Lord to baptise you with the spirit of a champion. You must pray the spirit of dominion and victory upon your life before going to bed every night. If evil spirits come to attack you in such a mood, they will experience defeat each time. You can command such demonic agents to consume the food which they bring you in the dream.

Never go to sleep in an angry mood. Those who go to bed after a sharp disagreement or a serious fight cannot escape being attacked in their dream. You must also avoid going to bed in a depressed state of mind. Those who go to bed discouraged always find that they are attacked in the dream.

Demonic agents are very clever. They watch your mood and build their attack on the platform of any frame of mind that runs contrary to the word of God.

Read the Scriptures that are capable of making you imbued with a sense of victory as you go to bed. If you can saturate your mind with the word of God when you are about sleeping, you will prevent night visitors from visiting you.

Do not read dirty books or watch dirty films. Those who read dirty books will invite spiritual attacks when they sleep. Those who watch horror films or demonic late night movies are responsible for spiritual attacks in the realm of the dream.

Ask God's angels and His hedge of fire to surround your

place of abode before going to bed. The angels of God are supposed to protect you when you go to bed. God expects you to activate them every night by simply issuing a word of command. You should also surround yourself, with God's hedge of fire. Failure to issue this command may invite demonic attack from the camp of the enemy.

Anoint your body and your bedroom periodically if you have suffered demonic attacks previously. You must anoint your body with anointing oil regularly. You should also anoint your bedroom to prevent demonic infiltration.

Seek the help of the Holy Spirit. This step must be taken by you if you often forget important dreams. Ask the Holy Spirit to remind you of the details of the dream.

Deal with any instance of demonic attack. If demonic agents attacked you in the dream, you must counter such attacks by going into fervent warfare prayer. As soon as you wake up in the morning, anoint your body and pray aggressively. You must send all arrows back to the senders. You must not allow any instance of demonic attacks in the realm of the dream to frighten you. God has given you enough weapons with which you can overcome every attack from the pit of hell.

You must make use of defensive weapons to quell all insurrections against your life. God does not expect you to cringe before the devil. He expects you to match him fire for fire. That is why the Bible says, "Resist the devil and he will flee from you."

Deliverance From Spirit Husband and Spirit Wife

Now I want you to stir up the anger in your spirit as you get ready to deal with the enemies of your soul. The devil has done enough damage in your life. Now is the time to face him squarely and tell him: "Satan, enough is enough. I will no longer allow you to toy with my life." You will not know what it means to spoil the works of the devil until your heart is filled with anger against the evil which satan and his hosts have perpetrated in your life.

The only language which the devil understands is the language of spiritual violence. The devil has done enough damage in your life. You must face him with fierce anger and holy wrath. You must turn the prayer session below to weapons of revenge. Now is the time to deal with spiritual armed robbers and compel them to restore whatever they stole from any department of your life.

Pray as if this is your last chance to force the devil to return whatever he stole since you were born. You must cry like blind Bartimaeus. Now is the time to shout at all spiritual thieves. Do not stop praying until you have a witness in your heart that you have entered into the realm of dominion and recovery of what the enemy stole from your life.

Seek a divorce from all spirit wives or husbands. Sack all evil night caterers. Severe every link with demonic agents. If you can say the prayer points at the end of this book, you will have testimony upon testimony until your life becomes an un-ending testimony.

CHAPTER SIX

The Night Raiders

There is an important aspect of spiritual warfare which has been neglected by the global company of prayer warriors.

Many prayer warriors have not been able to deal with powers that attack men and women in the night.

People have suffered terrible problems and received the greatest attacks at night. A lot of people who were healthy, happy, sound and normal went to bed in the night only to wake up with mysterious sicknesses, mental disorder, business failure, death of a loved one, collapse of marital relationships and other mishaps.

Unless you learn how to deal with night raiders, you will continue to go through some problems in life. The believers who know how to target and deal with these wicked night raiders will recognise that the root or the foundation of the problem will begin to shake. Evil powers will no longer be able to hold sway over your life. Satan's arrow will no longer penetrate your life. Long-standing problems will vanish and things that appear impossible in your life will become possible.

The average Christian loves peace. Most Christians pre-occupy themselves with seeking and pursuing peace. Nobody wants conflicts and hostilities. Most of us would like to go through a whole year without a single attack. That is a dream that will never come to pass. Whether we like it or not the devil has declared war against every one of us.

Every believer is in the battle field. To choose to fold your hands is to decide to become a casualty on the field. Even if you are not conscious of the fact that you are on the battle field, that does not exempt you from the warfare. Satan hates every one of us with perfect hatred. He is active every minute, fighting to destroy everyone who has relationship with God. You owe yourself the duty of fighting the battles of life and dealing with every attack that comes your way, either in the day or at night.

The activities of evil night raiders are exposed in four passages in the Scriptures. These passages unravel the mystery, the secrets, the strength and the weaknesses of wicked night raiders.

Matthew 13:25:

But while men slept, his enemy came and sowed tares among the wheat, and went his way.

Sleep is a very strong friend of the enemy. He has specialised in using sleep as a form of anaesthesia to perform evil operations on innocent men and women. He makes use of the cover of darkness as a cloak for attacking his victims.

Deliverance From Spirit Husband and Spirit Wife

He attacks people where they are weak, vulnerable and unprotected. He is conscious of the fact that the moment a person goes to bed he becomes unconscious and unable to resist attacks. That is why 90 per cent of the attacks which people go through occur in the night.

Have respect unto the covenant: for the dark places of the earth are full of the habitations of cruelty (Psalm 74:20).

This second passage is quite revealing. Here, reference is made to a realm that is hidden from human view, the dark places of the earth. This hidden realm is the habitation of wicked forces which operate in the night. The Bible makes it very clear that members of that evil society are cruel. Everything they do has a tincture of cruelty. Anything they do against individuals in the night is cruel and wicked.

There are regions of the universe which cannot be seen with our naked eyes. In parts of that invisible realm, lots of activities are carried out with the intent of unleashing cruelty upon men and women.

The dark places of the earth are found in every community. The community in which you live is filled with invisible powers whose task is to wait for the hour of darkness and attack men, women and children. For someone to become a member of that society, he or she must be a wicked person.

The Bible gives a vivid picture of some of the activities that take place in dark places in Job 4:12-14:

Now a thing was secretly brought to me, and mine ear received a little thereof. In thoughts from the visions of the night, when deep sleep falleth on men, Fear came upon me, and trembling, which made

133

Deliverance From Spirit Husband and Spirit Wife

all my bones to shake. Then a spirit passed before my face; the hair of my flesh stood up:

Job was attacked by a night visitor. Job did not bargain for what happened to him. All he wanted was sleep but he woke up the next day trembling and fearful. A spirit visited him. This made his hair to stand on end. That experience was embarrassing to him. The attack was so vivid that he trembled when he woke up.

We are given further insights into the activities of night raiders in Eph. 5:11:

And have no fellowship with the unfruitful works of darkness, but rather reprove them.

In this passage, emphasis is placed on what is done under the cover of darkness. The Bible says that those things are so bad that it is improper to speak about them. What evil powers do in secret is terrible. Only God can open our eyes to the reality of what happens in the spiritual realm.

Satanic night raiders have destroyed so many lives. It is nice when you are able to build walls around your house and put broken bottles or barbed wires on it. That is a very good effort. These satanic raiders do not need the doors of their victims opened to carry out their activities. They can go in and out of walls. They carry out their activities at all times and in all places, even when serious efforts are made to ensure security.

A friend of mine happened to be a senior military officer. In spite of all the efforts I made to share the gospel with him, he decided not to give his life to Christ. However, he was jolted out of his complacent state when he had a strange experience. He was sitting in his office one day, when a strange visitor entered, beating all security efforts put in place by this high ranking military officer. The strange visitor held his shirt and said: "Tell me, don't you know that I can kill you right now? Where are your body guards?" The military officer was thrown into confusion. The strange visitor spent a minute or two and went out.

The military officer felt that his body guards were careless and decided to charge them for dereliction of duty. He summoned all of them and the personal security staff and queried: "Why did you allow that man to pass through the security post to my office?" They wondered what the officer was saying. They told him that no human being passed through the security department. Again, he told them: "But the man left my office right now. Didn't you see him when he was coming out?" They answered him: "Sir, we are always standing at attention. It is impossible for any man to beat our security check point and come into your office. Nobody passed through this place." He couldn't believe them.

He told them again: "But the man came inside and spoke face to face with me." All the soldiers stood their ground saying: "Sir, that can never happen. Nobody can ever pass through this check point. It is impossible." It then dawned on the senior military officer that he had received a different kind of visitor. From that day, he gave his life to Christ and committed himself unto the only One who neither slumbers nor sleeps.

Deliverance From Spirit Husband and Spirit Wife

You have lots of invisible enemies who do not need to take permission from you before attempting to attack you. They operate under the cover of darkness. Unfortunately, you cannot see them, neither can you detect their activities. That is why I want you to close your eyes right now and take this prayer point:

Oh Lord, open my spiritual eyes, in the name of Jesus.

There is a testimony in one of our booklets, Power Must Change Hands, concerning a woman. The woman had a. friend whom she thought was a true friend. The woman dreamt of a cow coming to attack her in her dream and decided to share that dream with her closest friend, who opted to take her to a particular man of God. The woman was surprised by what the man of God said. Instead of saying anything to the woman who had the dreams, the pastor faced the friend who brought her and said: "Let me warn you, you must stop your evil work. If you attack her again, God will deal with you." Her friend simply said: "Yes sir, I have noted what you said, I will comply."

The woman kept on praying asking God to intervene in her situation. One night, the cow came as usual to attack her. However, the woman had learnt to pray fervently. Her prayer point before she slept that night was: "Let the Rock of ages smash my opposition." Just as the cow was about to hit the woman, a mighty rock came between her and the cow and the cow crashed on the rock, fell down and died instantly. Early the next morning, neighbours came knocking at her door to tell her that her friend died that night. They also told her that there was a very big wound on the head of her friend, as if someone had hit her with a big stone. That was how God gave the woman victory over her unfriendly friend.

Once again I want you to close your eyes and take this prayer point:

Oh Lord, open my spiritual eyes, in the name of Jesus.

A friend of mine had a very strange experience when he imported some goods. One of the items disappeared mysteriously. He ransacked everywhere but could not find the item. But God gave him a revelation after he had prayed. As he slept, God took him to one of the warehouses at the seaport. God told him: "Go to the left, to the right and to the left again and look under a particular table." He did and to his surprise, he found the missing item there. When he woke up, he went to the office of the clearing agents and boldly asked them: "Where is the missing item?" They told him that they had tried their best but could not find it. He told the agents that the good was in one of the warehouses and that he knew the particular spot where it was.

They laughed at him saying: "What are you trying to say? We have not found the missing item. We have tried our best. The item is nowhere to be found." He insisted that if they would allow him, he would fetch the item from where it was hidden. The clearing agents flared up saying, "Are you trying to say that we have stolen your item? We have told you that the item is nowhere to be found. Now, we are going to allow you to search for it but if you cannot find it, we are going to prosecute you for libel." The man told them that they should prosecute him if he failed to bring the item from where it was hidden. The man was so bold that because God had given him a clear revelation.

The brother asked the clearing agents to follow him as he followed exactly the same direction given to him in the dream. He turned to the left, to the right and to the left again and behold, there was a table. He bent down and brought out his item. It was hidden there by someone who stole it and wanted to take it away when nobody would be around. All the clearing agents were embarrassed.

Another friend of mine also had a strange experience when he decided to hire new staff. Twelve people turned up for the interview. My friend had soaked himself in prayer before the day of the interview and God opened his eyes to see beyond the physical realm. To his surprise, he saw the applicants in very strange postures. Some of them were sitting on their heads, others were hanging in the air while some were hiding under the table.

Out of the twelve people, only one was free spiritually. He quickly decided to cancel the interview. "Gentlemen, this interview has been cancelled due to certain reasons beyond our control. You are free to go back home. Just leave your addresses behind and we shall get in touch with you if necessary." As people were going out one by one, he pulled the coat of the only one who was spiritually free and told him to wait behind for a brief chat. He later interviewed him and decided to employ him. That was how God saved him from

Deliverance From Spirit Husband and Spirit Wife

employing wizards who would have ruined his new company.

Several years ago, when I was a young Christian, I had an unusual experience. A creature that looked like a gorilla appeared beside my window. I thought I was dreaming, opened my eyes and the gorilla was there. I closed my eyes and it was still there. Then it became clear to me that a night raider had come to visit me. The creature opened his mouth to announce where it came from. Then I went into an aggressive prayer session and the evil creature disappeared.

That was how I dealt with that evil night raider.

You must close your eyes at this moment and take this prayer point:

Every night raider, be disgraced, in the name of Jesus.

Did you take that prayer point? I want you to repeat it now with some slight variation:

Every night raider, be disgraced right now, in the name of Jesus.

WHY NIGHT RAIDERS OPERATE IN THE NIGHT

Night raiders carry out all their activities in the night because darkness provides a good cover for their evil activities. It is clear that the night is characterised by darkness. Here are the characteristics of darkness.

Darkness is the absence of light.

Darkness is not a positive creation. It is the consequence of the absence of the sun.

Deliverance From Spirit Husband and Spirit Wife

Darkness is the result of obscuring light. It comes up when light is hindered from penetrating into a particular place.

People find darkness uncomfortable because of the uncertainty of the environment where it is.

Darkness can cause a person to lose his way.

Darkness can make a person to expose himself unconsciously to danger. For example, if there is a snake in a dark room which you cannot see, you will expose yourself to danger.

Darkness causes a person to wander about.

Darkness causes an individual to stumble. Men easily stumble when they find themselves in darkness. That is why the Bible says "Give glory to the Lord your God, before he calls darkness and before your feet stumble upon the dark mountains, and while you look for light he turned it to the shadow of death and made it gross darkness" (Jeremiah 13:16).

There are degrees of darkness - We have partial darkness, medium darkness and gross darkness. For example, if you decide to illuminate a large building with one candle, you will have partial darkness, but if there is no light there at all you will have total darkness.

Darkness is silent - There is a lot of silence in dark places.

Darkness has a binding power - It binds people and limits their activities. Whenever there is darkness, you are confused. You don't know where or how far you can go.

Deliverance From Spirit Husband and Spirit Wife

Darkness has separating power - The introduction of darkness causes division.

Sleep takes place mostly at night. At that time, every evil takes place. Your best friend may turn around to harm you under the cover of darkness. The devil has released an army of night raiders upon the sons of men. The night is the most conducive time for evil powers to carry out their evil activities. A lot of evil things take place at night.

Sacrifices, robbery, witchcraft attacks, demonic meetings, disco parties and other evil things take place at night. If you have observed properly, you would have observed that most of the things which people find difficult to do during the day are done in the night. If you survey all the evil activities that are done in your community, you will observe that most of them are carried out in the night.

This shows that the night is meant for works of darkness. Most drinking places, drug joints, disco houses and other places where men and women carry out nefarious activities are generally active in the night. I hope there is no true believer who runs a beer parlour. Anyone who does that and calls himself or herself a believer is living in self deceit. Any believer who sells alcoholic drinks is also joking with hell fire.

Most criminals go about in the dark hours of the night. Most witchcraft meetings are held at night. Generally speaking, iniquity flourishes in the night.

WHO THE NIGHT RAIDERS ARE

Marine powers - They carry out their activities in the night. Many of them are found in the streets at night. They roam the streets as ladies looking for men who will give them lift. Unfortunately, some foolish men enter their traps, not knowing that they are carrying strange entities to their homes. When a single lady who is below 25 decides to stand alone under a dark bridge at about 1:00 a.m., looking for lift, she cannot be an ordinary person. An intelligent man should know that a lady must have some extra powers for her to stand there alone without fear at that time of the night. She must be a creature of the night herself.

Something normally happens during some night parties. The moment it is mid-night, some extremely and unnaturally beautiful ladies appear at such parties. It is often difficult to identify them. They come in without being invited. Some men quickly rush to them not knowing that they are delegates from the marine world. They are part of the company of the evil night raiders.

Familiar spirits - These forces go about confusing men and women, causing disasters, initiating people, distorting people's lives, causing demotion and fuelling the power of household wickedness. The strength of these powers lies in the fact that they are thoroughly familiar with their victims. They are able to carry out their evil activities because the secrets of their victims are known to them.

Witchcraft powers - These powers are well-known to

Deliverance From Spirit Husband and Spirit Wife

Africans. Although witches and wizards are somehow active during the day, they carry out most of their activities during the night. The hours of the night are their finest moment. As men and women lay down their weary bodies, witchcraft powers settle down to work by destroying lives and property.

Forest demons - These powers sometimes move out of their domain and mix up with men and women. Those who find themselves in the forest in their dreams are part of the victims of the night raiders.

Wandering spirits - These spirits wander about looking for people to possess.

Evil angels - These powers go about like normal human beings, only to disappear whenever their identity is about to be known. Just as there are good angels, there are also bad or evil angels. The good thing about good angels is that a single angel can destroy thousands of Satan's angels. For example, one angel of God destroyed 185,000 Assyrians in the Bible.

Satanic angels - These are fallen angels. They are wicked angels who double as men and angels and deal with human beings.

Wicked personalities - These wicked personalities carry out wicked assignments. Recently, a strange woman was caught in a posh area in Lagos, Nigeria. She was upturning people's dust bins in the neighbourhood searching for something. Once she realised that she could not find what she was looking for, she would turn the contents back to the dust bin. Then she would go to the next dust bin. Unknown to

143

her, somebody was watching her from a distance.

The person watching her suddenly realised that she was excited whenever she found a used menstrual pad in a dust bin. The observer saw she put the pad in her handbag and resumed her search. The observer recognised that she was looking for nothing but used menstrual pads. She was gathering as many used pads as possible. No doubt, she was carrying out an evil assignment. It was clear that she wanted to use peoples' sanitary pads to do something against them.

Occult powers - Lodge members, Free masons and other occult groups hold their meetings at night.

Spirit wives and spirit husbands - These forces go about at night raiding innocent men and women.

Ancestral strongmen - These spirits arrest people in the night.

Recruitment agents - These powers recruit or initiate men and women into all kinds of evil societies.

Spirits impersonating the dead - Some spirits impersonate dead people. It is because of these that there are reports of dead people who are seen in real life.

Satanic spies - These spies work like spiritual intelligence officers. Their task is to gather information concerning people which they take back to the Satanic kingdom.

Counterfeit angels - These forces pretend as if they are angels of God while they are not.

Dream manipulators - They manipulate people's dreams.

Deliverance From Spirit Husband and Spirit Wife

The Eaters of flesh and drinkers of blood - Their task is to destroy and cause all kinds of health problems.

Spirits from the second heavens - The second heaven is the heaven where darkness reigns. Spirits from that realm go about destroying peoples' lives.

Night caterers - They feed people with evil meals in the dreams at night.

The demon of pestilence - The Bible has stated that pestilence moves about in the night.

Local masquerades - They are part of the company of the evil night raiders.

Demon idols - These idols are sent to pursue and attack men and women.

Household pursuers - These powers operate within the household and attack members of the family.

Spirits of death and hell - These spirits also operate in the night. They are killer spirits.

Can you imagine what happens when these 24 powers decide to attack human beings? Unfortunately, there are people who are attacked by forces from more than 15 groups.

Now close your eyes and take this prayer point? *Every activity of satanic night raiders, be frustrated, in the name of Jesus.*

CHARACTERISTICS OF THE NIGHT RAIDERS

They are persistent - They have great determination and

Deliverance From Spirit Husband and Spirit Wife

zeal. They are always at their duty posts. They avoid offending satan their cruel task master. They have compiled a list of all our weaknesses and use them as points of persistent attacks.

They are persuasive - They persuade people to carry out ungodly assignments. They push men and women to do what will make it easy for evil powers to attack them.

They are punctual and committed - They are always on time. If demons visit a particular person at 1.00 a.m. they will never be late. They do not miss their hour.

They are liars and deceivers - They show you all kinds of things in order to deceive you.

They are very productive - They always achieve maximum success. If these powers are not succeeding there will be no need to have deliverance ministers. Every night raider is a specialist. It knows how to do the right thing at the right time.

They are powerful in their own right - The Bible says: "When I was with you daily in the temple, ye stretched forth no hand against me but this is your hour and the power of darkness" (Luke 22:53). Here, Jesus admitted that powers of darkness have their own kind of power. However, although they are powerful, their own power is inferior to ours.

Today, a lot of people experience night visitations. Some are tired of these visitations but do not know what to do. Others keep the experience to themselves. These powers try to visit everyone. They do not want to give people breathing space. Their purpose is to kill, steal and destroy.

You may not be able to prevent evil powers from attempting

to visit you, but you must not allow their weapons to prosper in your life. These powers visited Jesus but failed. Unfortunately, today, the weapons of the evil night raiders are prospering in the lives of so many people. Very few people are victorious over these night raiders.

Some people are helpless whenever they are attacked by raiders at night. Some are so weak that they cannot call the name of Jesus when they are attacked. Some people would fight battles until they wake up in the morning. They become tired as if they had fought a real battle.

I do not know how many blows you have received from such night raiders. It is possible to experience victory at the end of a night raid only to wake up the next day with a swollen face. I am sure you know that there are some boxers who win in a boxing tournament only to be hospitalised for one week after the fight. That is why you must not joke with any encounter with night raiders. Therefore, I want you to take this prayer point.

Every satanic visitation at night assigned against my life, fall down and die, in the name of Jesus.

I have heard stories of people who go to bed hale and hearty only to experience a cold chill suddenly. Unless you know how to pray, the cold chill may continue for some time before it stops. You may then conclude that everything is over. You may not know they have planted something in your life. If you wake up the next day and rush to see a doctor, the doctor may prescribe some drugs for you but nothing will be able to take away the sickness because it is a spiritual attack.

Deliverance From Spirit Husband and Spirit Wife

There are those who are healthy only to suddenly receive an attack of paralysis all over their bodies. That is not an ordinary sickness. Others experience a swelling without knowing why. Sometimes some people observe that their heads become larger than usual. It is an evidence of an evil attack. Others are pressed down by some unseen forces when they are asleep. Some people would almost pass out because some unseen forces choked their throat. Others experience attacks from masquerades. Some are shot by uniformed soldiers in the dream.

If you have ever had a dream in which you were shot by soldiers take this prayer point: *I fire back every satanic bullet, in the name of Jesus.*

A lot of people suffer from attacks of night raiders by receiving evil visitations from demon idols. Demon idols are short or small in stature. They are harsh and stone-faced. They go straight for their victims and attack them. Sometimes, they would not take human form but sometimes when they attack there is no physical evidence of their presence. But in the form of a wind, their victims would feel a sharp pain in their body.

Recently, a lady shared a testimony with me. She was invited to a meeting and strangely, the only vacant seat was given to her. She sat down not knowing that some powers had planned evil against her. She sat down not suspecting any foul play.

Suddenly, something was fired from the seat into her body.

She was afraid. Fortunately for her, she heard the voice of the Holy Spirit "Don't let that arrow get to the region of your head." She promptly obeyed the instruction. What saved her was the fact that she was a prayer addict who always went about with her anointing oil. She stood up from her seat and rushed into the toilet, opened her bag, brought out the anointing oil and anointed her head. That was how God delivered her from that evil arrow. If she had not obeyed the voice of the Holy Spirit, she would have died on the chair and passed to eternity.

Victims of night raiders have all kinds of experiences. Some of them hear strange voices without seeing any human being. Others find themselves arraigned in a court in their dreams. Others dream and find themselves among a company of people in black uniform. If you do not pray about that kind of dream, you might be initiated forcefully into the demonic society.

Some of these night raiders are so effective that they do not have to touch their victims before planting evil objects in their lives. I wonder if there is anyone who has never had a visit from these night raiders at one time or the other.

If you have noticed that you are stagnant instead of breaking new grounds then you can be sure that night raiders are at work. If you have noticed that your dream life is a war front, night raiders are at work. If you have noticed that you always have one funny dream or the other whenever you are about doing something that is very important then you must be aware of the fact that night raiders are fighting against you. If being attacked in the dream makes you to experience automatic failure in real life, you do not need anyone to tell you that night raiders are carrying out some wicked activities in your life.

WHY NIGHT RAIDERS PROSPER

The power of God has not changed. It has never and will never fail. The problem is not with God but with us. You may ask: Why should night raiders prosper in the life of a child of God? The reasons are obvious.

Sin - Night raiders have legal rights over those who are living in sin, to trespass and attack them. So, if you are living in sin, you are exposing yourself to attacks from night raiders. If you have sex outside marriage, you are destroying yourself and throwing an invitation to night raiders.

Curses in place - Night raiders carry out their activities wherever they find unbroken curses in people's lives.

Evil covenants - Evil covenants are fertile ground for operation by evil night raiders.

Evil properties - Evil properties may include stolen goods, demonised objects which could be your earrings or your shoes, cursed art works and other materials. Such goods attract night raiders.

Lack of deliverance - Whenever there is incomplete deliverance or lack of deliverance in your life, evil powers will attack you.

Bad spiritual environment - If you happen to live in an

environment that is spiritually contaminated, you are likely to experience evil visitations from night raiders. Or if you live in a place where sin abound, you will be opened to attacks.

Backsliding - When you talk about backsliding, some people think of those who have turned their backs at God. That is not true. A backslider is anyone who fails to follow the Lord wholeheartedly. Those who refuse to obey the word of God, or allow sins in their lives, those who are crooked in their dealings with others, those who turn back to the devil, those who forget God and those who have left their first love and are now lukewarm.

If you deny Jesus as Peter did, look back like Lot's wife, or are stagnant in your spiritual life, you are a backslider. You must settle your account with God today.

The only way you can be free from evil night raiders is to totally surrender your life unto God. If you allow evil night raiders to gain access into any department of your life, you will be attacked. Get rid of everything that invites evil powers into your life today. Pray until you are free from every attack of night raiders.

CHAPTER SEVEN
DISGRACING SPIRIT WIVES AND SPIRIT HUSBANDS
(Incubi and Succubi)

Release from Evil Spiritual Marriage

The supernatural world is as real as the physical. What takes place in the spiritual realm affects us physically in our day to day lives. Ignorance is no excuse. The fact that you are not aware of a bad situation does not mean that you will not suffer its consequences.

It is unfortunate that some people go through terrible situations in life while remaining in darkness as regards the source of their problems. A lot of people beat about the bush without knowing the cause of their sufferings and problems. They ignore the root of their problems and search for solutions where none exists. The greatest good you can do to yourself is to go back to the root. Your present problems might have been caused by supernatural forces.

Deliverance From Spirit Husband and Spirit Wife

You must ask the Holy Spirit to open your heart to the realities of the supernatural world. That may be the beginning of your miracles. By and large, you will discover that certain yokes, covenants and evil linkages must be dealt with in your life if you must live a happy, holy, healthy and prosperous life.

The subject of the evil spiritual marriage has been grossly mis-understood by many people. While some hold erroneous views, others demonstrate partial knowledge of this all-important subject. What we are considering in this chapter goes beyond the popular concept for spirit husbands and spirit wives. It goes beyond that point and teaches the evil of succubi and incubi actions. The problem of evil marriage goes beyond dilettantish purposes.

Evil marriage is a deep subject. It affects many people. From our spiritual research and statistical findings, we have gathered that seven out of ten ladies who profess to be born again are involved, consciously or unconsciously, with evil spiritual marriage. In the same vein, seven out of ten Christian men are also consciously or unconsciously affected by evil spiritual marriage.

If you gather ten ladies together and ask them questions about their dream experiences, their marital lives and certain mysterious happenings in their lives, you will discover that they are involved with spiritual partners or husbands.

The easiest index is this: If you have ever had an immoral affair with anyone who is not free in every sense of the word, then you can be sure that your relationship, as simple as it appears, has led you into a spiritual relationship. It is difficult to know those who are free from those who are not? Even if you have never been involved in any immoral act, you are still targeted as a possible wife or husband to those who have little or pronounced association with demonic powers.

You may be surprised to know that a spirit wife or a spirit husband may fancy you and decide to use his or her spiritual power to lead you into a spiritual marriage which you may never be conscious of. The world in which we live is more complex than we can ever imagine. That is why, it is never safe to take anything for granted.

As you read this book, it will benefit you if you make up your mind to be a believer rather than a doubter. If you have a genuine problem along this line, you will save yourself heartaches, unpleasant experiences and enigmatic situations if you decide to deal squarely with it. You will not have lost anything at the end of the day. Even if you did not have this kind of problem at all at least, you are now aware. Your prayer would still be used by God to bless you and set you free from all kinds of hidden covenants or curses.

If you have listened to the kind of stories which I am bombarded with on daily basis, you would have no room in your heart about the existence of extra-human powers which try to get involved with innocent human beings. Now, if the issue of evil spiritual marriages can be that serious in the church, then it is far worse outside the church. In other words, if the righteous is scarcely free what is the fate of the ungodly?

Deliverance From Spirit Husband and Spirit Wife

To understand the true situation in the secular world, question your unsaved neighbour and he or she would tell you that, there are lots of deep experiences which cannot be understood by man. Some of them would tell you that, evil personalities come to them as ladies or men to violate or abuse their bodies while they watch helplessly. Surely, something is wrong somewhere, it is an undeniable fact. It is a universal human experience.

There are no questions as to the source of evil spiritual marriage. Undoubtedly, the devil is the head of all evil spiritual marriages - simple or complex. This explains why majority of those who are involved with evil marriage are kept in the dark concerning their dangerous physical and spiritual states. Satan is generally more effective when his victims are totally ignorant of what they are suffering. That is why there are people who have remained in an evil spiritual marriage fc. 20 or 30 years. Sad enough, some people bear the yokes to their last days on earth.

This is a subject which no one can afford to dismiss with a wave of the hand. It is worthy of consideration by every sincere and serious-minded person.

Evil spiritual marriage is more complex and real than many people would imagine. Unfortunately, it is a legal marriage, even though it is contracted in the spiritual realm. The results are visibly in the physical realm. We are aware that legal contracts are binding for those who are involved in it. Those who are legally married in the spiritual realm but have no inkling of the reality of the marriage are to be pitied.

Deliverance From Spirit Husband and Spirit Wife

A man or a woman, who is bound under the law to fulfil certain conditions but fails to do so, will face the consequences whether he or she likes it or not.

In 1992, a Christian sister came for counselling and narrated a strange experience which she had. She told me of a strange marriage which she contracted with a strange man. The marriage was real. However, she was not conscious of the fact that it was more than a physical marriage. She did not know that she was married to a man who was not an ordinary human being. That was the first time I heard such a strange story.

She brought a family photograph which she showed me. She said that right from the first day of their marriage, the man kept telling her that if she ever gave her life to Christ or joined the Jesus people, she would look for him and would never find him. The woman never took him serious. She always joked about it asking, "What do you mean? How dare you make yourself an enemy of God? You must be kidding." She thought he was joking. Everything went on smoothly with the family until the day she gave her life to Christ. She never suspected anything until she got home only to find that her husband had disappeared mysteriously.

To make matters worse, everything concerning the man had vanished. That was not all. Their four kids also disappeared. They were nowhere to be found. She did not know what was going on until it dawned on her, later, that she had married a spirit being. Her story really surprised me but the evidences were right before me. I saw her wedding photographs and those of her four kids. She had married a spiritual husband and given birth to spiritual children who vanished the moment she violated the law of the evil spiritual marriage.

This kind of story may sound strange to many people especially the academic or intellectual minds, those who believe in only what can be seen, tasted, felt, handled and proved empirically. Some theologians may also doubt the reality of evil supernatural marriage. They may opine that we must prove such ideas theologically. They refuse to accept whatever does not agree with their theological school of thought. They relegate the supernatural to the background and emphasise theological knowledge while battling secretly with the problem of evil spiritual world and marriage.

I have come across theologians who find it difficult to get married at the age of 40 and above, when their problems are simply rooted in their involvement with spiritual wives or spiritual husbands.

Therefore, many cases abound of innocent sisters who wake up every day to realise that they were sexually molested or abused by strange men in their dreams. They become confused and begin to get angry with themselves. Sometimes, their days are affected negatively by such sexual dreams. Others find it difficult to get husbands.

An elderly woman came to me sometime ago complaining that she had been unemployed for a very long time. However, she got a job after she was prayed for. She felt highly elated. She was so excited that she looked forward to her first day in the office.

On the night preceding her first day, she had a strange dream. She found herself in the midst of a wedding ceremony. Strange enough, she was the bride. It was a church setting. She saw the congregation, the pastor and a bridegroom. She found herself standing side by side with an unknown man and was supposed to be joined together with him in marriage. The whole situation seemed bizarre to her.

In that dream, she called the strange pastor and said, "Who is this man? I'm sorry I don't know him. What kind of strange wedding ceremony is this? Why must I get married to a strange face? Count me out of this wedding." The Pastor ignored her statement and continued conducting the strange wedding ceremony. She decided to run for her life. That was how she ran out at the middle of the service. The pastor, the bridegroom and the rest of the congregation ran after her. She woke up tired and fearful.

She did not understand the implication of such a dream until she resumed work the following day. Expecting to be shown the way to her office, she was shocked when they told her to hold on for an hour or two. She was later called into the office of the director who told her, "Madam, we are sorry to have wasted your time. Although we gave you a letter of appointment, we have discovered that we made a mistake. That letter was not meant for you. Please, forget about the letter of appointment. You can try your luck elsewhere. Goodbye."

Deliverance From Spirit Husband and Spirit Wife

It was as if the ground should open up and swallow her. She felt humiliated, confused and tired. She ran back to me to narrate how she lost a job she had just secured. She narrated her strange dream. I told her what to do. I instructed her to summon the strange congregation, the evil marriage partner and the strange pastor who was trying to conduct the wedding, renounce every form of involvement with such an evil gathering and destroy all satanic agents associated with it with the fire of the Holy Ghost. She carried out the instructions.

She went back to the same company which had rejected her. The director apologized profusely and gave her the job immediately. That was how she had a positive change in her life after dealing with evil spiritual marriage.

SCRIPTURES ON SONS GOD

How real is evil spiritual marriage? Is it scriptural? Let us take a journey into the scriptures.

And it came to pass, when men began to multiply on the face of the earth, and daughters were born unto them, That the sons of God saw the daughters of men that they were fair; and they took them wives of all which they chose (Gen. 6:1-2).

Let us reflect briefly on this passage. Here we are told that 'the sons of God' saw that the daughters of men were fair. What is the significance of that statement? Just as a man sees a lady and she is fascinated or attracted to her, so a spirit being can admire a normal human being and decide to strike a compulsory marriage deal with her.

Deliverance From Spirit Husband and Spirit Wife

Let us examine Gen. 6:4:

There were giants in the earth in those days; and also after that, when the sons of God came in unto the daughters of men, and they bare children to them, the same became mighty men which were of old, men of renown.

Who are the people referred to here as the sons of God who married the daughters of men? Some people opine that they refer to the fact that the children of Seth in the Bible went to marry the children of Cain. We must explain Scriptures with Scriptures and allow the usage of biblical words to be clarified by parallel passages in the Bible.

SONS OF GOD

The terminology sons of God appear only five times in the Old Testament in Genesis 6:1-4:

And it came to pass, when men began to multiply on the face of the earth, and daughters were born unto them, That the sons of God saw the daughters of men that they *were* fair; and they took them wives of all which they chose. And the LORD said, My spirit shall not always strive with man, for that he also *is* flesh: yet his days shall be an hundred and twenty years. There were giants in the earth in those days; and also after that, when the sons of God came in unto the daughters of men, and they bare *children* to them, the same *became* mighty men which *were* of old, men of renown.

The same Hebrew expression is used in Job 1:6 and 2:1, describing '"When the sons of God came to present themselves before the LORD, and Satan came also among them." Angels are clearly of interest here, as is plain from the only other occurrence of the term 'sons of God' in the Old

Deliverance From Spirit Husband and Spirit Wife

Testament:

> Where wast thou when I laid the foundations of the earth? declare, if thou hast understanding. Who hath laid the measures thereof, if thou knowest? or who hath stretched the line upon it? Whereupon are the foundations thereof fas tened? or who laid the corner stone thereof; when the morning stars sang together , and all the sons of God shouted for Joy? (Job 38:4-7)

Without doubt God is referring to angels rejoicing at creation. So, if the term refers to angels here, and the same Hebrew words are used in the other two passages in Job and in Genesis 6, then the term "sons of God" is an Old Testament designation for angels.

So, we have good angels rejoicing at creation and presenting themselves before God in the days of Job; and we have fallen angels who sinned with the daughters of men in the days of Noah - both of which are known as "sons of God."

Old Testaments use of "sons of God"

The expression -'sons of God' is found only five times in the Old Testament, twice in Genesis 6 and three times in the book of Job (1:6; 2: 1; 38:7). The passages in Job clearly refer to angels. Furthermore, the account of Shadrach, Meshach and Abednego in Daniel 3:24-25 calls an angel the son of God. In Jude 6-7 we read

> The angels which kept not their first estate, but left their own habitation, he hath reserved in everlasting chains under darkness unto the judgment of the great day. Even as Sodom and Gomorrha, and the cities about them in like manner, giving themselves over to fornication, and going after strange flesh, are set forth for an example, suffering

the vengeance of eternal fire.

If Sodom and Gomorrah and other cities committed fornication 'in a like manner' as the angels, then it is clear that the sin of angels was fornication. According to Genesis 6 this sex sin was committed with the 'daughters of men.'

Let us briefly look again at Job 1:6:

Now there was a day when the sons of God came to present themselves before the LORD, and Satan came also among them.

This passage shows that the sons of God were angels. This meeting did not take place on earth. It has nothing to do with the children of Seth. It refers to angelic beings.

Job 38:4 says,

Where wast thou when I laid the foundations of the earth? declare, if thou hast understanding.

This passage makes it clear that the sons of God were angelic beings not normal human beings. The people referred to as sons of God who came to daughters of men and committed immorality with them. These angelic beings, otherwise called sons of God, were fallen angels. This is made clear in Jude 1:6:

And the angels which kept not their first estate, but left their own habitation, he hath reserved in everlasting chains under darkness unto the judgment of the great day.

What did these angels do to warrant such judgement? Verse 7 gives us the clue:

Even as Sodom and Gomorrha, and the cities about them in like manner, giving themselves over to fornication, and going after strange flesh, are set forth for an example, suffering the vengeance of eternal fire.

It is clear that these angels were doing things that were similar to what was done in Sodom and Gomorrah: fornication and sexual immorality.

If we now combine all the scriptures in the books of Genesis, Job and Jude, we shall gain insight into the existence of certain demonic beings who go into relationship with human beings.

Everything was perfect at the beginning. There were no fallen angels or demons. But satan later fell and drew the support of one-third of the angels of God. Satan and his angels fell from their elevated position and were cast out of heaven. The devil became the enemy of God while his angels became fallen angels. They were no longer the sons of God as before. Or, if you like, they were fallen sons of God.

The incident in Genesis chapter 6 took place after the fall of man. That is where we come across the first instance or the first mention of the incident of evil marriage between human beings and demons or spirit beings. Just as children were produced from that evil union, those who are involved with evil spiritual marriages today equally have children in the spiritual world. Such demonic children inhabit the earth, the sea and the sky above.

The example we have just given illustrates one form of the operations of spirit beings which lead innocent people into evil marriages. There are other operations and manifestations. The same spirits which operate in the book of Genesis

Deliverance From Spirit Husband and Spirit Wife

sometimes take up the appearance of men. They come as men to attack women thereby becoming their spirit husbands. They also come as women to attack men thereby becoming their spirit wives. This shows us that many people are married in the spiritual realm.

35 FACTS ABOUT ANGELS

1. They are mentioned 306 times in the Scriptures. The word 'angel' is mentioned 202 times and the word 'angels' 104 times (KJV Bible).

2. They were all created by God. *Gen. 2: 1; Neh. 9:6; Eph. 3:9; Col 1:16.*

3. They were present at the creation of the world. *Job 38:1, 4, 7.*

4. They are not to be worshipped. *Col. 2:18; Rev. 19:10.*

5. They report directly to God. *Job 1:6; 2:1.*

6. They announced Jesus' birth to the shepherds. *Luke 2:10-14.*

7. They do not marry. *Matt. 22:30.*

8. They are spirits, like the soul of man, but not incorporeal. *Ps. 10; Heb. 17:14.*

9. They were created to live forever. *Luke 20:36.*

10. Their purpose is to glorify God. *Rev. 4:8.*

11. Some angels help human beings. *Heb. 1: 14.*

12. Some angels harm human beings. *Mark 5:1-5.*

Deliverance From Spirit Husband and Spirit Wife

13. They are spirit beings. *Ps. 104:4; Heb. 1:7, 14.*

14. They are invisible beings. *Rom. 1: 18-32; Col. 2:18; Rev. 19: 1 0; 22:9.*

15. They are innumerable. *Deut. 33:2; Matt. 26; Heb. 12:22.*

16. They rebuke idolatry. *Judg. 2:1-4.*

17. They possess superhuman intelligence and power. *Mark 13:32; Ps. 103:20; Dan. 9:21-22; 10:14; Rev. 19:10; 22:8-9.*

18. They possess intelligence. *Dan. 9:21-22; 10:14; Rev. 22:8-9.*

19. They appear to man in human form. *Gen. 18:2; 19:1,10; Acts 1:10.*

20. They possess will. *Isa. 14:12-15; Jude 6.*

21. Imperfection is ascribed to them as creatures. *Job 4:18; 1 Pet. 1:12.*

22. They display joy. *Job 38:7; Luke 2:13.*

23. They display desire. *1 Pet. 1:12.*

24. They are stronger than men. *Ps. 103:20; 2 Thess. 1:7; 2 Pet. 2:11.*

25. They are more intelligent than men. *Dan. 9:21-22; 10:14.*

26. They are of different orders. *Isa. 6:2; 1 Th. 4:16; 1 Pet. 3:22; Jude 9; Rev. 12:7.*

27. They are elect. *1 Tim. 5:21.*

28. They are examples of meekness. *2 Pet. 2:11; Jude 9.*

29. They are swifter than men. *Dan. 9:21; Rom. 14:6.*

30. They are not omnipresent. *Dan. 10:12.*

31. They are not omnipotent. *Dan. 10:13.*

32. They are not omniscient. *Matt. 24:36.*

33. Some are cherubim. Ezek. 1: 1-28; 10:20 .

34. Some are seraphim. *Isa. 6:1-8.*

35. The majority remain true to God. They will join all believers in the heavenly Jerusalem. *Rev. 5:11-12 27 Heb. 12:22-25.*

VARIOUS FORMS OF EVIL SPIRITUAL MARRIAGE

Conscious evil spiritual marriages - Some people are aware of the fact that they are involved in evil spiritual marriages. They are consciously involved in what is happening in their lives.

A brother once gave a challenging testimony on how he experienced victory over the evil spiritual marriage. According to him, a particular strange being came to him every 4:00 a.m. at a particular day. The lady, who was light-complexioned and attractive, would come and lay down by his side. Whenever she came, he was helpless. It was clear to him that certain powers usually took control of his will. He compulsorily went into sexual immorality with the lady until he was tired and exhausted.

By the time it was day break he became useless, confused and sick. That went on for years. However, the situation changed when he learnt how to pray fire prayers. He was

Deliverance From Spirit Husband and Spirit Wife

able to solve the problem because he was conscious of what was happening.

Those who are unconscious of their involvement with evil spiritual marriage - For those who are unconscious of their involvement in spiritual marriage, the problem exists all the same. If these people can examine themselves, they will discover that they have a problem. If you find yourself thinking about immoral things or if you find yourself in strange sexual behaviour, that may be a sign of unconscious involvement in an evil marriage

Those who are forced into evil spiritual marriage - people in this category are forced into sexual intercourse or raped in their dreams.

Those who can see their spiritual spouses physically - Those in this group are not ignorant of what is happening in their lives. Sometimes they can identify their spirit husbands or spirit wives physically. Whenever they are in a particular place, they can see their spirit wives or spirit husbands while others who are there cannot see these strange beings.

A strange event took place years ago during a wedding ceremony. The bride and the bridegroom were standing by the altar waiting to be joined together. The officiating minister turned to the bride and said, 'Will you take this man as your lawfully wedded husband and keep to him? ...' The priest waited for an answer. The woman said, 'No.' The church was thrown into an uproar. The priest felt that he did not hear her properly. He repeated the question, 'Will you take this

man as your lawfully wedded husband and keep to him? . . .'
Before he finished, the woman said an emphatic 'No.'
Everybody was surprised.

Initially, the pastor did not know what to do. The
bridegroom was equally nonplussed. The priest could not
continue. All of a sudden he turned to the congregation and
said, 'Ladies and gentlemen, since the bride has stated before
us all that she is not ready to get married to this man, can we
continue this wedding ceremony by asking for volunteers? I
am sure that the bridegroom will not mind getting a new bride
right here.' Before he finished, three ladies rushed forward,
signifying their intention and readiness to marry the man.
Quickly a choice was made among the three ladies. That was
how the man got married to a different lady.

What was the problem of the original bride? She had a
spirit husband who would not allow her to be married.
Unknown to the officiating priest, the bridegroom and the
entire congregation, immediately the lady was asked, 'Would
you marry this man?' her spirit husband stepped forward and
told her 'If you ever open your mouth to say yes, you will die
on the spot. You are married to me forever. You can never
marry any human being.' This strange voice was heard only
by the woman. The woman recognised her spirit husband
and his presence was more real to her than the presence of
the physical bridegroom. Even when the bridegroom pleaded
with her passionately to say yes, the presence of the spirit
husband was so intimidating that she could not.

Those who cannot see their spirit wives or spirit

Deliverance From Spirit Husband and Spirit Wife

husbands physically - Although people in this category cannot see their spirit wives or spirit husbands physically, yet they somehow know that they are involved in an evil marriage.

Those who have international spirit wives or spirit husbands - There are also international spirit wives or spirit husbands. Those who are involved with them are conscious of their experiences. One day, they dream about having sex with an Indian, the next day they dream about a white man or a white lady. Some other time, they come across a black spirit wife or spirit husband.

Those married to local spirit wives or spirit husbands - These satanic agents sometimes take up the appearance of someone who is very close to you, for example your husband, wife, or brother in the physical realm.

Those involved with evil spiritual marriages - These are marriages in which dowries are fully paid and there is a ceremony.

Those in courtship - These categories of people are not yet married. They are still courting. The involvement is not total or complete.

Those who are not too serious with the evil spiritual relationship - In this case the commitment is not very deep. The spirits involved here are just floating around, messing people up. They go about as playboys or spiritual flirts messing up whoever they come across. They are not looking for stable wives or stable husbands. They appear and

169

disappear.

Those involved with monogamous spiritual relationships - Some men or ladies are married to one spirit wife or spirit husband. Those spirits are so powerful that they cannot allow any other spirit to have any affair with their earthly wives or husbands.

Polyandrous and polygamous evil marriages - One lady can be a wife to as many as five spirit husbands while one man can be a husband to several spirit wives. Some of these wives could come from the sea, others from the rock and some from the air. The spirit wives take their turns. That is why some ladies dream about three men fighting over them. It also explains why some men dream about sleeping with two or three spirit wives at the same time. The men are never able to have any meaningful marriage on earth because spirit wives are generally jealous and possessive.

Normal human beings who decide to use demonic or occult power to attack a lady or a man who refuses to marry them - When some wicked men or women meet someone they like but who incidentally refuses their advances, they go into astral projection in the night to sexually molest her or him.

From what you have read so far, you can see that the problem of evil spiritual marriage is not an ordinary one. Why don't you take a short break and say this prayer point?

Every unprofitable linkage, I break you by fire today, in the name of Jesus.

Now that you are aware that evil spiritual marriages are real, you must also know how to detect the occurrence of such ugly situations in your own life or in the life of anyone around you.

INDICATIONS OF INVOLVEMENT WITH EVIL SPIRITUAL MARRIAGES

Unclean dreams - Whenever you have dreams of sexual intercourse, it is an indication that you have a spirit husband or spirit wife. Sexual intercourse is only normal among married partners who have the experience in the physical realm. For anyone to have sexual intercourse in the dream means that such a person is married (consciously or unconsciously) to a spirit being. Sometimes, the person dreams of contracting marriage with a known or unknown person. If you continue to have these kinds of dreams, marriage may become impossible in the physical realm. It is worse when a woman finds herself giving birth to a baby in the dream.

Difficulty in child-bearing - These spirits interfere with marriages, making child-bearing impossible. When they allow their victims to give birth to children, they ensure that such children are abnormal or useless to their parents. Or the children may end up being agents of demonic attacks. Such children may make statements like, 'We are responsible for the lack of progress in the family. The sickness which has drained the family purse was caused by us.'

Deliverance From Spirit Husband and Spirit Wife

Confusion and uncertainty - These spirits are also responsible for creating confusion in the hearts of young men and young women. Sometimes you hear of ladies who have accepted marriage proposals only to turn back to say no as a result of confusion and uncertainty.

I have received hundreds of letters from men who are complaining of inability to find a lady to marry. I have often wondered why such men are suffering in the midst of plenty. The reason is that some of them have been involved in invisible marriages with spirit wives who are extremely jealous and would not allow them to get married to an earthly woman. If such a man insists on marrying any lady, the spirit wife would descend on the lady.

Disharmony - If someone with a spirit wife or husband succeeds in getting married, he or she hardly lives to enjoy the marriage. They experience strange things in their marriages. The situation is worse when both partners are involved with a spirit wife and a spirit husband. The spirit wife would fight against her rival while the spirit husband would fight against his rival.

In any marriage where the partners are quarrelsome, argumentative and irritable, they are suffering from the activities of spiritual husbands and spiritual wives.

It is clear that spiritual wives or husbands are marriage destroyers. They hate the institution of marriage with perfect hatred. They want the marriage to break. If you visit any divorce court, you will see that marriages are dissolved. As

Deliverance From Spirit Husband and Spirit Wife

high as 90 per cent of the problems are caused by spirit wives and spirit husbands.

Many years ago, I met a woman in a street near our church. She was indeed a strange sight to behold. She was carrying all kinds of funny household utensils: pots, spoons, plates, brooms, pillow, lantern, palm oil keg, clothes, etc. It was a massive load. To make matters worse, a baby was strapped to her back. She was walking in the heat of the sun. Although I did not know her, I had to call her, 'Madam, what is happening? Why are you carrying such a heavy load this sunny afternoon? Where are you coming from and where are you going?' I invited her to the church.

This was when I was a young minister. Her reply was embarrassing: 'Don't mind that stupid man who calls himself my husband. He is a mad man. I am tired of living with him. I have just decided to pack my belongings and go to live with my aged parents. I am sure I will have peace of mind if I live with my parents.' I told her that she was wrong. After talking with her I asked her to go and apologise to her husband. She did, and they were re-united. But why did the woman leave her husband's house in the first place? Spirit husbands and spirit wives were responsible. They did not want her to live in her husband's house.

Some of these evil spiritual wives and husbands can kill if they become very angry. They are very cruel in their jealousy. Sometimes you come across some cases in which wives are wrongly accused by their real husbands. They tell such innocent women, 'Madam, I want to announce to you that

Deliverance From Spirit Husband and Spirit Wife

you are a witch and that you are the one who is responsible for all my problems.' What is responsible for such statements? Maybe the man had a dream in which he was attacked by someone who came in the appearance of his wife. When he wakes up, he would accuse his wife, without knowing that it was a jealous spirit wife who wanted to cause a conflict, or if possible, a total breakdown in their marriage. The wife is not a witch. It is simply the manipulation of wicked spirit wives. On the other hand, the woman might take offence and decide to move out of her husband's house, without knowing that that was the intention of the jealous spirit wives. That is how many marriages have been destroyed.

Spirit wives and husbands block good things from coming to the family. Their goal is to make life as difficult as possible.

Attack through female menstruation - Any lady who is careless with her period may be in serious trouble. Remember that life is in the blood and access to your menstrual blood by the enemy can cause up to 20 problems for you. Let me recount to you the testimony given by a sister about four years ago.

After a prayer session entitled: 'Know the Secret,' a sister was shocked to receive a visitor from her home town, who knelt down before her and started begging for forgiveness. 'I do not recall that you have wronged me,' responded the sister. This woman then said, 'I have been restless for the past one week and this is why I come all the way to Lagos to look for you. I took your menstrual pad about 20 years ago to a shrine to prevent you from getting married and bearing children. After the rituals, I hid the menstrual pad inside a cracked wall. This is why you have found the issue of marriage and child-bearing problematic. Please, forgive me.'

The sister dismissed her. Later, when she travelled home she found a dusty old menstrual pad inside the cracked wall. She took it out and burnt it. This was how she received her breakthrough.

The strategy of some evil people is to steal a woman's menstrual pad or to find out the dates of her menstrual period.

Then the spirit of the owner of the menstrual pad is invited at night and the menstrual pad is shown to her to confirm ownership. Thereafter, the menstruation becomes irregular and the sister may start putting on some demonic weight.

For total manipulation of menstruation, it is required that someone brings the sand on which the sister has urinated. The first recognisable sign is intense stomach-ache during menstruation or at irregular periods. May the good Lord deliver us from those watching us while we are unconscious of it.

The problems from local evil attack through female menstruation manifest as:

• Irregularity.

• Protractedness.

• Barrenness and miscarriage.

• Contaminated children.

Deliverance From Spirit Husband and Spirit Wife

- Problems in obtaining a partner.
- Husband's lack of interest in the family.
- Prostitution.
- Breast cancer.
- Things moving around in the womb.
- Dreams of blood leading to miscarriages.
- Covenants with spirit husbands.
- Wrong choice of husbands.
- Unexplainable constant sicknesses.
- An uncontrollable sexual urge.
- Family unrest and divorce.
- Development of polygamous tendencies by husband.
- Unexplainable internal heat.
- Severe headaches during menstruation.
- Menstruation may cease totally.
- Prolonged pregnancy.

These are popular local evil arrows. Since many sisters are always careless about their menstrual period, they easily become victims of these local attacks.

Solution

- Pray for divine revelation to enable you to expose the problem.
- Pray to withdraw your blood and urine from any evil altar.

Deliverance From Spirit Husband and Spirit Wife

(Use our book 'Pray Your Way To Breakthroughs,' or use the prayer points at the back of this book.)

• Cancel the effect of evil attacks through the menstrual period.

• Pray to recover what the enemy has stolen from you.

Attack through the male seed or sperm - Any man who sleeps with a woman, married or single, outside marriage, is digging his own grave. This is why the Bible has these deep statements recorded in 1Cor. 6:15-19:

Know ye not that your bodies are the members of Christ? shall I then take the members of Christ, and make them the members of an harlot? God forbid. What? know ye not that he which is joined to an harlot is one body? for two, saith he, shall be one flesh. But he that is joined unto the Lord is one spirit. Flee fornication. Every sin that a man doeth is without the body; bun he that committeth fornication sinneth against his own body. What? know ye not that your body is the temple of the Holy Ghost which is in you, which ye have of God, and ye are not your own?

You might have "joined yourself" to a harlot many years ago. Your sperm may be under the sea now. Most women who offer cheap sex in the streets are agents from the water sent to destroy men. They are sent from the sea and have 12 basic areas where they entice men for sperm collection:

• Hotels.

• Universities.

• Secondary schools.

• Hair-dressing saloons.

• Betting offices.

177

Deliverance From Spirit Husband and Spirit Wife

- Markets.
- Cinema halls.
- Night clubs.
- Dead churches. (Especially where the leaders have many wives.)
- Night parties.
- Car-lifts (rides).
- Beauty shows/contests.

May the good Lord have mercy on sisters whose husbands' seeds have been captured and stored beneath the water.

This has caused a lot of problems for men. Even if the male seed was collected as far back as when you were in the secondary school, you may still have some battles to fight now. Here are some of the problems that may accompany such attacks:

- Constant sexual relationship with spirit wives.
- Low sperm count or none at all.
- Total financial collapse.
- Hatred by the opposite sex.
- Inability to find a good wife or none at all.
- Sticking with a demonic girl, no matter how hard he tries to get out of the relationship.
- Everything such a person touches will only prosper if he does not see or use water.
- Regular sexual dreams.

Deliverance From Spirit Husband and Spirit Wife

- Ceaseless masturbation.

- Intense sexual thoughts.

Foolish sisters who employ girls of 25 and 26 years as house girls may be trapping their husbands.

Also, sisters should check their friends who visit when they are not at home and only when their husbands are at home.

Solution

- Complete repentance and prayers for forgiveness.

- Submit yourself for deliverance ministration or consult our book on 'How to Obtain Personal Deliverance.'

- Pray to withdraw your semen from evil altars.

- Pray to cancel whatever evil it has been used to do.

HOW SPIRITUAL WIVES AND HUSBANDS ARE ACQUIRED

How are these spirits acquired? How do men and women get into evil spiritual marriages? What are the avenues for such unnatural incursion into the institution of marriage?

The greatest problem we face today is that people find themselves in very complex situations and it is difficult and it seems impossible for them to disclose what they are going through. Some who disclose their problems are often embarrassed by the reaction of the people they confide in. Such counsellors, or pastors often make statements like, 'You mean this is what has been happening to you? Your case is very difficult. I have never come across this type of problem.

Deliverance From Spirit Husband and Spirit Wife

I cannot promise any help. If I decide to help you, the spirits who are attacking you will focus their attention on me. You must be a strange fellow. Please, do not ever let anyone hear what you told me. I do not think that there is any solution to your problem.'

What an ungodly response to a genuine problem. That is why only very few people talk about their problems today. The majority are afraid of telling anyone the details of the mysterious things they are going through.

A member of our church had an experience which baffled her. A neighbour came to her house because she had the strange problem. The sister heard a knock at her door and got up to welcome the visitor. Behold, it was a pregnant woman. She welcomed the woman and asked her to sit down. The woman narrated her problem. 'Sister, I have a problem and would like to confide in you. I am sure you have never come across my kind of problem but, please, I need your help. I want you to take me to your church.'

The Christian sister wondered what the problem was, looked at the woman and said: 'Don't worry, I will take you to the church. But what exactly is the problem? Tell me so that I can know how urgent it is.' Then the woman asked the sister to put her ears near her stomach. The sister almost ran away when she heard the baby in the woman's womb talking. The sister said, 'Please, I am coming. In fact, I was almost going to see someone just before you came in. I am sorry, I won't be able to take you to the church. The address is No. 13, Olasimbo Street, off Olumo Road, Onike, Yaba. I advise you to go immediately. Please, don't wait any longer. In fact, I would like to close the door of my house right now.'

The woman was still trying to ask more questions concerning the location of the church but the sister only said, 'Just go, you won't miss it. Goodbye.' She was happy that she had been able to push away a strange woman. What kind of baby was that? Why should a baby talk in the womb? It sounds strange, doesn't it? What do you think would have happened if that woman's husband had heard the words of the strange baby? Won't he ask the woman to take her belongings and go away?

Seeking satanic protection - If you have ever sought for protection from agents of the devil, you may end up getting involved with evil spiritual marriage. Let me make this very clear. There is nothing like ignorance in the spirit world. If you are ignorant, you will pay dearly for it. Those who go for protection in questionable places usually get more than they bargained for. You may end up with an evil spiritual marriage.

Many innocent young girls have been given away in marriage to evil spiritual forces. How does it happen? Maybe when the girl was a baby, she was taken to a prayer house or to the shrine of a fetish priest, where a bangle was put on her legs as a means of securing her life. No doubt, such power may prevent her from dying, but it will go beyond that. The bangles may be used as an instrument of giving her away to an evil spiritual husband.

Other young girls or babies have incisions in all parts of their

181

bodies. Some are dedicated to powerful idols to ensure that they are protected from untimely death. These powers may protect the babies from death but they may have to pay a very high price for the protection.

These evil powers may make up their minds that the young girls they have protected would become their wives for life. Such girls may then find it difficult to get any men to propose marriage to them when they grow up. Their parents wanted protection but they ended up getting spirit husbands for their children. This explains why a lot of marriageable men and women are finding it difficult to meet anyone who is genuinely interested in them. Such people should check their foundation and cleanse every spiritual contamination if they want to experience breakthroughs in every area of their lives.

Immorality - The Bible says:

Know ye not that your bodies are the members of Christ? shall I then take the members of Christ, and make them the members of an harlot? God forbid. What? know ye not that he which is joined to an harlot is one body? for two, saith he, shall be one flesh (1 Cor. 6:15).

It is clear that the moment anyone goes outside the bounds of marriage, such a person is open to satanic contamination. A lot of men and women have got into problems this way.

Satan is very clever. He sets clever traps for careless people. If you allow the devil to blindly lead you into immorality with a possessed lady, you may end up contracting marriage with her in the spirit realm. You will not know that such a spiritual marriage is real until you pray fervently. Then, the spiritual power behind the evil marriage will react. If you argue too much, they may tender the spiritual marriage certificate as an evidence against you.

Unprofitable gifts - A person may be entangled with an evil spiritual marriage through the acceptance of gifts. Today, many people are unconsciously married to spirit husbands and spirit wives because they received certain gifts. If you receive cheap gifts from people, you may be collecting objects of initiation into ungodly spiritual marriages.

If a man gives a present to a lady and the man happens to be an evil agent, the lady will surely marry the spirit behind the man. If you received a gift from a demonic man when you were a sinner, and now that you have become born again you think that everything is over, you are wrong. It is when you intend to get married that such a power will fight you. He will succeed in his effort because you actually collected a gift from him.

Recently, we had to pray for a lady who had serious problems. She was a very beautiful lady but her life was a bundle of complicated problems. The first man who approached her for marriage landed in the hospital after a serious fight. His skull was fractured. He managed to survive, opted out of the relationship and ran for his dear life.

Soon afterwards, another man came her way. The man was so interested in her that he promised to marry her. Again there was a serious fight between them. The man survived the fight but lost an eye. The lady had used broken bottles to remove his eye. That was the end of the relationship.

Deliverance From Spirit Husband and Spirit Wife

A third man came, who proved to be difficult. A fight also came up. But that man fought it out with her, being a demonic agent himself. She broke the man's head and the man also broke her head. Then, she discovered that she had a great problem. She decided to go for deliverance. The deliverance minister took time to find out what her problem was, but she did not disclose anything. However, things took a different turn when the minister said, 'You demons, if you have refused to let her go because of the gift which she had collected from you, I break the link between both of you and I command you to let her go, in the name of Jesus.'

All of a sudden the demon in her screamed, 'I am coming out but she has to fulfil a condition. She must return the wrapper which she collected from us. Then, I will have nothing to do with her again.' The minister had to destroy the wrapper and whatever it represented before she was set free. Have you collected any gift from agents of satan? You may have to return such unprofitable gifts if you must experience freedom.

Cultural dances -

And when Aaron saw it, he built an altar before it; and Aaron made proclamation, and said, To morrow is a feast to the LORD. And they rose up early on the morrow, and offered burnt offerings, and brought peace offerings; and the people sat down to eat and to drink, and rose up to play (Exo. 32:5-6).

If you were involved in cultural entertainment and dancing, in the village or in an urban area, you have probably got involved with a spiritual marriage. The local idols have their

184

altars. If you dance before such idols you might become a bride or a bridegroom to them.

Check the lives of those who are involved in traditional dances. You will realise that they are not spiritually free.

Inheriting satanic priesthood - An average African family has a family idol. These idols are inherited from our ancestors. Some of the idols have been worshipped by generations for hundreds of years. Various objects are worshipped by different families. Some people worship snakes, some worship coconut trees, while some worship other trees. Although we live in a modem age and many of these idols have been destroyed or thrown away because of civilization, the links with them have not broken.

Families have priests who minister to the family idol. What does a 'priest' mean? It basically means marriage to a deity. That is why many African priests and priestesses refuse to marry. They are already married to the deity whom they worship. Anyone who worships an idol is married to that idol. That is why those who worship the Lord Jesus, are called the bride of Christ.

There are two kinds of priests. Some priests are well-known as devotees of certain idols, while others appear like ordinary human beings. There are also priests in the spiritual realm. That is why you should not take certain things for granted. If someone comes to your house and jokes with your children saying, 'This is my wife. This is my husband.' If such a person is a priest, he can lead your child into evil

185

spiritual marriage.

Recently, a man was sick to the point of death and was summoned to his village by his parents. He was taken to a bush at the back of the family house where there was a huge black stone and was told to perform some rituals. The priest simply asked him to repeat the following words, 'Oh deities, I have come to you today because I need your help. I am going to get married to you if you can solve my problem.' The man repeated what the high priest said and was instantly healed. But that was not the end of the story. He also became married to the deity. One problem was solved only for a greater one to be ushered in.

Soul ties - Many people get into spiritual marriages through ungodly soul ties. If you have ever had a demonic boyfriend or a demonic girlfriend, whom you gave your photograph, this may lead to soul-tie and eventually to a spiritual marriage.

A sister once came to me to make a funny request. She said, 'Here are the names of seven men. I am planning to marry one of them. Please, make the right choice for me. But please, note that the first two are prosperous and wealthy. Both of them have cars. The other five are still struggling. When can I come for feedback?' I looked at her and gave her a piece of my mind. I told her that I would not be involved with such a foolish exercise. I would not choose marriage partners for people. I also challenged her by saying, 'You are covetous. What are you doing with the names of seven men? You must sort yourself out. You need deliverance.' The truth did not go down well with her so she ran away from me.

Deliverance From Spirit Husband and Spirit Wife

Eventually, she decided to marry the richest among them. Her home was like hell on earth. The man almost killed her. But surprisingly, she could not get out of the relationship. Her parents advised her to get out of the man's house to avoid being killed. She agreed with her parents and attempted to return to her parents, only to run back to the wicked husband the next day. This situation persisted until it dawned on her that the husband was not an ordinary human being. She decided to confront him. It took her a lot of courage to do so. Finally, she faced him.

'I have decided to talk to you today because I am tired of all your wicked actions towards me. I have evaluated our relationship and come to a conclusion. You are not a normal human being. Your behaviour towards me suggests that you are not free spiritually. You cannot deny the fact that you are a demonic agent and I think you are planning to kill me.' The husband looked at her, smiled, and said, 'Oh, I pity you. I thought you knew that you have been married all these years to a demonic husband. I am not free. I have never been free. To tell you the truth, you have been married to two of us. I am a dual personality. I am your physical husband but there is another being who is always with me. You are also married to that spirit being. That is why I have sometimes beaten you to the point of death. You are suffering under the wickedness of two satanic agents.'

The woman opened her mouth and could not close it. All she managed to say was: 'I know that Jesus will deliver me from both of you.' She was indeed funny. Why did she want Jesus to deliver her when she did not, in the first place, allow the Lord to lead her to the right partner?

Unholy sexy dresses - Seductive dresses lead ladies into evil spiritual marriages. Any dress that reveals delicate parts of your body may drag you into an evil marriage. If you advertise your body through highly suggestive and tight-fitting dresses, you may also attract the attention of spirit husbands. That is why women who dress carelessly and seductively hardly have stable homes. They find it difficult to stay with any husband because they are involved in a marital relationship with spirit beings.

If a lady dresses as if she was coming out of the water, putting on clothes with wet looks, she may attract the attention of husbands from the marine world. Evil spirits are easily attracted by seductive dresses.

Covenants with first sexual partners - Unknown to most people, they enter into evil covenants with the first lady or man with whom they had sexual intercourse. We all know that when a virgin has an affair with a man, blood is involved. This may lead to a spiritual marriage. You can then imagine the number of evil spiritual marriages and demonic problems certain men who have slept with many virgins would have had.

Masturbation - A lot of people take certain things for granted. For instance, some go into masturbation not knowing that they are opening themselves up for satanic attack and bondage. Such people do not know that what they are doing have both physical and spiritual implications.

Circumcision - Circumcision is an age-long practice in many parts of the world. In many communities, both the male and the female are circumcised. The problem, however, is that the type of person who performs the rites of circumcision determines whether the person circumcised will get into an evil spiritual marriage or not.

Sexual perversion - Abnormal sexual practices like homosexuality, lesbianism, bestiality, oral sex, anal sex, etc. are channels through which people are led into evil spiritual marriages.

SOLUTIONS

What then are the solutions to all these problems? How can you get out of evil spiritual marriage if you are already involved in it? What must you do to regain your freedom?

Repentance - The first step you must take is to repent of all sins in your life. Repentance has always been the key to liberty and freedom from bondage. Repentance is not a modern concept. If you refuse to repent, you cannot experience deliverance. Repentance leads to freedom. Repentance must be thorough and must cover every area of your life.

Go before the Lord to settle your account with Him.

Deliverance From Spirit Husband and Spirit Wife

You will call a spade a spade. You will list out, as many as you can remember, all the men or ladies with whom you have been involved. You may have to itemise all the instances and thoroughly repent of them. Then you must go ahead to break every covenant which you have with all those sexual partners. General confession of sin will not help in this area.

Identify and locate the entry points of these spirits.

Make atonement by the blood of Jesus - You may have to pray in this manner: *I plead the redemptive power in the blood of Jesus. I redeem myself with the blood of Jesus. I set myself free from every evil marriage by the blood of Jesus. I use the blood of Jesus to wipe away every evil marriage relationship.*

Reject and renounce every evil marriage - You must remember that every evil marriage is legally binding on those who are involved in it. The Bible says,

And Jesus answering said unto them, Do ye not therefore err, because ye know not the scriptures, neither the power of God? For when they shall rise from the dead, they neither marry, nor are given in marriage; but are as the angels which are in heaven (Mark 12:24-25).

This passage shows us that God does not approve of any attempt by any spirit to go into marriage. Spiritually speaking, it is illegal. The Bible makes it clear that species should reproduce after their own kind and Scriptures cannot be broken. Here is what another Scriptures says 2 Corinthians 11:2,

Deliverance From Spirit Husband and Spirit Wife

For I am jealous over you with godly jealousy: for I have espoused you to one husband, that I may present you as a chaste virgin to Christ.

With this Scripture you can challenge all illegal marriages. Tell every spirit wife or spirit husband: Jesus is my divine spouse. He is jealous over me with godly jealousy.

Issue a bill of divorce - As soon as you have rejected every evil marriage you are free to issue a bill of divorce against them.

Bind and cast them out of your life.

Command every spiritual deposit to depart from your body.

Execute judgement upon them - Let me end this chapter with Psalm 149:

Praise ye the LORD, Sing unto the LORD a new song, and his praise in the congregation of saints. Let Israel rejoice in him that made him: let the children of Zion be joyful in their King. Let them praise his name in the dance: let them sing praises unto him with the timbrel and harp. For the LORD taketh pleasure in his people: he will beautify the meek with salvation. Let the saints be joyful in glory: let them sing aloud upon their beds. Let the high praises of God be in their mouth, and a two edged sword in their hand; To execute vengeance upon the heathen, and punishments upon the people; To bind their kings with chains, and their nobles with fetters of iron; To execute upon them the judgment written: this honour have all his saints. Praise ye the LORD.

You must deal with every evil spiritual marriage today. Those who are married but are suffering from spirit

Deliverance From Spirit Husband and Spirit Wife

husbands and spirit wives can join hands with their husbands or wives and bring their real marriages before God. Then they can go ahead to destroy every evil marriage. If you are ready to take all of these steps, you will experience deliverance and freedom from the power of wicked spirit husbands and wives. The Lord will set you free. You will be free to live a normal life.

CHAPTER EIGHT

Flesh Must Die

The greatest enemy of man is on the rampage.

This enemy has disguised himself, pretending to be a friend. Sadly enough, the enemy has been accepted, pampered and celebrated. As a result of all the alluring attractions which he dangles before men, he has been offered a seat and crowned as king. This enemy is the devil. Yes, the devil is on the rampage. He does not come with fearful looking horns on his head. Rather, he comes through a bait- something that is acceptable to us - the flesh. It is our greatest problem.

This is the area where many of us have been defeated. Except you know how to handle the flesh, you cannot understand what the Bible calls abundant ljfe. You can operate on the minimum level and be satisfied. You cannot understand how sweet it is to serve the Lord until you deal with the flesh. If you do not want to become a permanent deliverance candidate, you must deal with the flesh. The flesh must receive a devastating blow.

The Bible says,

If any man will come after me, let him deny himself, and take up his cross daily and follow me (Luke 9:23).

Three keys assist us in understanding what it takes to follow Jesus:

One - deny yourself.

Two - take up your cross daily.

Three - follow Jesus.

The Bible says, "If any man". That leaves nobody out. Everyone is included, whether you are educated or not, tall or short, handsome or ugly. The Bible simply says, "If any man." The call of Christ goes out to every individual and you owe yourself a great duty to heed that call.

To heed the call of Christ, you must deny yourself. To deny yourself means you should forget about yourself. It also means to forget yourself in the hands of God. To follow Christ, you must be ready to lose sight of yourself, and must renounce yourself. The Bible says in 1 Corinthians chapter 15:31:

I die every day.

Paul, the great apostle, chose to die daily because the flesh constitutes a great hindrance to godly living. The flesh is the man within us who seeks to control our affairs. The flesh holds a powerful influence and is in constant rivalry and conflict with the spirit.

Its place of abode is the head where it controls, enforces, dictates, manipulates, whispers, tilts and influences its host. It is the way of life which we inherited from Adam. For example, you do not have to teach a child how to steal or tell lies. It is a natural thing to do evil.

The flesh does not always come up in a negative way. There are times when it takes up some positive manifestations. It may sometimes bring you money, fame, position or one form of worldly advantage or the other. But whatever it does, there is always a negative intention behind it. If the enemies of our lives were not harboured by the flesh, there would have been no problem of satanic attacks. Every deliverance minister would have been jobless.

The flesh is that part of man which is in rebellion against God. It is the evil entity within each human being that propels him to go against his maker, God. The Bible calls the flesh various names in identifying the various shades of its character. The Bible calls it, "sin in the flesh." It also calls it the "old man." It calls it, "sin which dwells within." Again it calls it, "every evil present within". It refers to the flesh as a "different law."

The flesh is that recalcitrant old man which forbids the practice of everything that is spiritually sound in the life of the believer. When the believer says, "I am going to be holy. I will read my Bible regularly. I will pray and fast fervently," the flesh will raise up every conceivable opposition.

Mr. Flesh is that being which produces action of self-satisfaction. It is the key that the devil uses to gain control over lives. The flesh is the producer of evil works. This is exactly why repentance amounts to the destruction of the works of the flesh.

The flesh is the fountain head of all sins. All sin emanates from the flesh. Anger, impure thoughts, lust, adultery and fornication are evidences of the fact that the flesh is on the throne. You may be free from particular sins, but the flesh is ruling your life through some other types of sin. You are not totally free.

The flesh operates a very effective satanic division of labour. There are fleshly agents in the area of sexual immorality. They handle a particular department of temptation. There are also fleshly agents in the area of speech and those who are responsible for lying, cursing, exaggeration and so on.

Again there are those that are responsible for the sins of the heart like pride, malice, envy, jealousy, evil thoughts, anger, etc. So, the flesh gives out various assignments in order to send the sons of men to hell fire. Lying or fornication, selfishness or anger, are fellow instruments in the workshop of the flesh.

The flesh often comes with a powerful surge, when

least expected by careless men and women. The flesh can be likened to a mango tree. The fact that there are no fruits on it at a particular season, does not mean that it can no longer bear fruit. In the same vein, do not rejoice that the works of the flesh are not visible in your life at a particular season. Unless your repentance is genuine and your spiritual temperature is hot, you may discover that the flesh will rear up its ugly head any time.

The fact that the mango tree is not producing fruit now does not mean that the mango fruit is not there. It is just waiting for the season, a convenient season, when the environment would be conducive. Do not think that you are free from a particular sin because you do not have the tendency of falling into it. Do not think that you can never commit fornication or adultery. It might be because the environment is not conducive and that helps to control your eyes. Only God knows what you will do when a secret opportunity comes . That is why some respected believers or men of God have fallen into one abominable sin or the other.

The flesh waits eagerly for any opportunity to strike. It can be quiet for one year, but someday it may strike the unsuspecting victim. This is why a pastor can beat his wife and a sister can slap her husband after she had just finished personal evangelism. The flesh may put on a religious garb, yet it remains Mr. flesh. The flesh is that arrogant, disobedient, rebellious, sinful nature, that makes it difficult for men to put God in the right position.

197

Deliverance From Spirit Husband and Spirit Wife

This is the reason some people prefer to live by the flesh. Such can argue blindly over the Bible.

Recently, I told a sister not to wear trousers because of spirit husbands. She started to argue with me. It is very easy to argue and even win the argument. Often the flesh is behind such clever argument.

Something happened, many years ago when I was a school teacher. There was another teacher who was also born again. Somehow, he did not believe total separation from the world. Whenever I challenged him concerning the traces of worldliness in his life, he would explain everything away. For example, he was always fond of hanging some fashionable chains on his neck. I told him that such an action was an evidence of worldliness; he disagreed.

However, something happened in the school which shook him to his foundations. A 15-year-old class three student walked up to him and said: 'Teacher, I just want to say that I love you.' He replied: 'But I am your teacher. Do you know the meaning of what you are saying? What kind of love are you talking about?' She replied: 'You are free to take any decision but whether you like it or not. I love you. There is nothing you can do about it.' He tried to flog her, then on a second thought he dropped the cane and rushed to me to narrate his strange experience. He said: 'Something strange is happening to me. The more she says she loves me the more I fall in love with the tiny girl. Is she trying some evil power on me?'

It was then he decided to listen to me and receive counsel on what should be the Christian's attitude to the world.

The flesh is not submissive to the will of God. It wants to be noticed. It does not want to be embarrassed. When it receives insults, it reacts negatively. It is the flesh that causes people to commit suicide, saying: 'It is better to die than to live a shameful life.'

The flesh gets angry wherever it is not congratulated. If you forget to acknowledge the flesh, it gets angry. Sometimes, inward anger may be concealed, waiting to be provoked again, that is the flesh.

When the flesh is accorded recognition and given an exalted position, it is happy. But put it under instruction, or supervision where it is unable to express itself freely, and it will feel bad. Does that describe your attitude?

Every little opportunity that the flesh has, it always wants to dominate.

It creates the tendency for you to think that you can do something without God. But the Bible says:

Trust in the Lord with all thine heart and lean not on thy own understanding (Prov. 3:5).

The flesh leans on its own understanding. It would always present worldly alternatives to the wisdom of God.

Two brothers boarded a bus and one of them was led

by the spirit to share the gospel with the people in the bus. The one who had the leading told the second brother to preach. The second brother refused because there were many ladies in that bus and he was ashamed of making grammatical slips before them.

However, the first brother stood up and preached a fiery message. God took control, the entire bus was electrified by the fire of the Holy Spirit. The second brother became jealous. He decided to stand up to preach an additional sermon. Was he led by the Holy Spirit? No. He was led by the flesh. Self was on the throne of his heart.

Self always wants to succeed. It does not want to fail. If the flesh goes out on evangelism and nobody gets converted, it becomes jealous of those who have gained some converts for the Lord. The flesh may even develop complete hatred for those who are succeeding. Those who live in the flesh would even down-play those who are successful in order to satisfy themselves and cover their shame.

The flesh does not want to be disgraced. The man of the flesh would rather borrow money than cut his coat according to his own cloth.

The flesh wants everybody to know that it is important and would ascribe glory to itself. A man of the flesh would want to ascribe glory to himself and take credit for everything.

The flesh is secretive. A man who lives his life in the flesh would not want anybody to know his secret.

I have a scientist friend who made a discovery that would have made him a billionaire. He discovered a tropical root in the bush which, when applied to crops would help to produce unusually large yields. He planted yams in a secret location and experimented the root on them. At the time of harvest, the yams were so large that the villagers ran away calling the tubers, demonic yams. As soon as he succeeded, he kept everything to himself. The only problem he had was that he could not identify the botanical name of the miracle root. So he sent a sample to an American botanist to help him identify the wonder-root.

He waited in vain for a reply. Two years later he travelled to America and discovered that the botanical expert had been able to find out the name and the uses of the root, but had decided to monopolise the discovery. That was how the Nigerian scientist lost the great opportunity. If he had shared his discovery with fellow Nigerian scientists, the case would have been different.

The flesh is always very defensive. It hates to be criticised. That is why the Bible says, "The flesh profiteth nothing."

Inability to control the flesh could send a lot of people to hell fire. You cannot experience revival in your spiritual life until Mr. Flesh is dead. As long as the flesh continues to rear up its head, you still have a long way to go.

Why don't you close your eyes at this point and pray this prayer point?

Every enemy of spiritual revival in my life, come out now, in the name of Jesus.

The flesh does not like to accept correction. If you fail to accept correction you will never grow. Students who hate correction can never become first class students.

'Self' is always ashamed of accepting blame, rather it is fond of shifting blames to others.

A general overseer friend of mine surprised me recently. There was a crisis in his church that involved his pastors. It was such a big crisis, that it almost resulted in a big fracas. He tried to mediate in the conflict but the pastors shouted him down. Patiently begging them to give peace a chance, the general overseer, who is far older than I am, prostrated before the 40 pastors and started crying. Then the pastors became overwhelmed. His action broke down every resistance in them. You may ask: 'But how can a general overseer prostrate before his pastors?' The answer is that he must have been dead to the flesh.

The flesh is greedy, and always wants to possess all. Women who are ruled by the flesh want to dominate their husbands at home.

Deliverance From Spirit Husband and Spirit Wife

Again those who try to hide their age are ruled by the flesh.

The flesh always likes to protect its own interests. It is pompous and proud. It can manifest its ugly characteristics whether in the classroom or in the marketplace. We often see the flesh in action in the church on the pulpit or in the choir.

The flesh likes to be alone. It likes to dominate, so as to be praised.. It avoids participation in group projects where its own effort cannot be singled out.

Some people break out from a big ministry like ours saying that God told them to go out. It is the flesh.

I know a brother who broke out of a ministry saying that God told him to start his own. He borrowed ₦10,000:00 from an unbeliever to hold a crusade. At the end of the crusade he was able to raise only ₦3,000:00. The unbeliever who lent him the money decided to embarrass him during a church service. The pastor became confused and ran to me asking for help. I wondered why he had to borrow money to hold an evangelistic crusade. Certainly the crusade was not sponsored by the Holy Spirit but by the flesh.

You will agree with me that something has to be done to the flesh for believers to be fervent for God.

· BE THE APPLE OF GOD'S EYES OR BE CRUCIFIED

God has reserved an exclusive class of those who have a special relationship with Him. This group of people are referred to as the apple of His eyes. When such people pray, they receive instant attention. What is their secret? They came to a point where the flesh and all its ugly characteristics are crucified, and the life of God is lived in all its entirety. What is referred to as the fulness of God, cannot be clear to you until flesh dies. You cannot enjoy the Almighty and share in His secret until self is crucified. The deep things of God cannot mean anything to you until the flesh is crucified.

The flesh is stubborn. It can only be tamed by the cross.

The Bible says:

And he bearing his cross went forth to a place called the place of the skull which is called in the Hebrew tongue, Golgotha and in Greek, calvary: (John 19:17).

The scene referred to in this passage took place on a mountain outside the city. The mountain looked like a skull. The first lesson we learn from this Scripture is that when you succeed in taking a man's skull from his head, you have killed him.

Another lesson is that crucifixion normally takes place at the outskirts of the city - an undesirable place.

Crucifixion entails going through shame, ridicule and

pains. Most people avoid crucifixion. The Bible says:

I am crucified with Christ: nevertheless I live; yet not I, but Christ liveth in me: and the life which I now live in the flesh I live by the faith of the Son of God, who loved me, and gave himself for me. (Gal. 2:20).

Here Paul the apostle declared without fear that he had been crucified with Christ, that the old man had died and that he had become completely new in Christ. Paul was saying that what took place in his life was not a refurbishment. It was a total transformation. He died and a new man emerged. How did this happen?

Let's look at the Scriptures again.

Blotting out the hand writing that was against us, which was contrary to us and took it out of the way, nailing it to the cross (Col.2:14).

And he that taketh not his cross and followeth after me, is not worthy of me (Matt. 10:38).

If you say that you are a Christian and you have not taken your cross to follow Christ, you are not worthy. That means that you are not qualified. In other words, you are disqualified. The Bible says:

Then said Jesus unto His disciples. If any man will come after me, let him deny himself, and take up his cross, and follow me (Matt. 16:24).

The Bible makes us to understand that the issue of crucifixion cannot be dismissed by a wave of the hand. It tells us again:

And He said to them If any man will come after me, let him deny himself and take up his cross daily, and follow me (Luke

9:23).

This is supported by another Scripture. Mark 10:21 says:

Then Jesus beholding him loved him, and said unto him, One thing thou lackest: go thy way, sell what-so-ever thou hast, and give it to the poor, and thou shall have treasure in heaven: and come, take up the cross, and follow me.

But what was the man's response? Verse 22:

And he was sad at that saying, and went away grieved: for he had great possessions.

Two of the songs that changed my life when I gave my life to Christ go like this:

Take up thy cross, the saviour said.
If thou wouldest my disciple be;
Deny thy self, the world forsake,
And humbly follow after me.

Take up thy cross, then in His strength
And calmly every danger brave,
'Twill guide you to a better home
And lead to victory o'er the grave.

Take up thy cross, let not its weight
Fill thy weak spirit with alarm;
His strength shall bear your spirit up,
And brace thine heart, and nerve, thine arm.

Take up thy cross, and follow Christ
Nor think till death to lay it down
For only he who bears the cross
May hope to wear the glorious crown.

Take up thy cross, nor heed the shame,
Nor let thy foolish pride rebel;
The Lord for thee the cross endured
To save thy soul from death and hell.

To thee, great Lord, the One in Three,
All praise for evermore ascend;
O grant us in our home to see
The heavenly life that knows no end.

Deliverance From Spirit Husband and Spirit Wife

O God, my heart doth long for Thee;
Let me die, let me die;
Now set my soul at liberty;
Let me die.
To all the trifling things of earth,
They're now to me of little worth,
My Saviour calls, I'm going forth,
Let me die.

Lord I must die to scoffs and jeers;
Let me die, let me die;
I must be freed from slavish fears;
Let me die.
Unto the world and its applause,
To all its customs, fashions, laws,
Of those who hate the humbling cross,
Let me die.

When I am dead, then, Lord, to Thee
I will live, I will live.
My life, my strength, my all to Thee
I will give, I will give.
So dead that no desire shall rise
To pass for good, or great, or wise,
In any but my Saviour's eyes;
Let me die, let me die.

To crucify the flesh, you must deny yourself. You will take a journey to Golgotha and be crucified. To be crucified means you are completely dead and are no longer alive.

A brother got on the bus and mistakenly stepped on a fellow passenger. Before he could say sorry to the aggrieved passenger, the man gave him a slap. Everybody in the bus urged the brother to retaliate. The brother smiled and apologised to the passenger. He said, 'I cannot slap him because my hands have been crucified with Christ.' The passengers looked at him and rained abuses on him. That is a crucified man.

THE CROSS

The cross stands at the centre of Christianity. Without the cross, Christian life is non-existent. Whatever runs contrary to the cross is not part of the gospel.

Christianity without the cross can be likened to a tree without fruit. The flesh does not want to be disturbed, yet it cannot co-exist with the cross. They are contrary to each other. Man is always looking for respectability, but the cross is the centre of God's glory.

The flesh loves what is fashionable a: d glamorous, but the cross is crude, old fashioned and ugly. Right through the history of the church, anytime the cross is relegated to the background, darkness sets in. Remove the cross and you weaken the church.

The cross cannot be forgotten or ignored. Even if all preachers refuse to preach about the cross, that will not remove its centrality in Christianity.

The cross is the soul of Christianity. It commands attention. There is something of an enigma in the cross.

The cross is a phenomenon. It is a mystery. It is the instrument of Christ's death and the object of wonder throughout all ages. It can never lose its power.

The power of God resides in the cross. When Christ was crucified on the cross, it was gruesome. The cross was first placed on His shoulder as a burden. He carried it to the place of crucifixion. He surrendered Himself for crucifixion. His two hands and two legs were nailed to the cross. This was a symbol of suffering. Unbelievers even identify the cross as a symbol of cross-roads.

You cannot avoid the cross and remain true to your conscience. I have made up my mind to surrender everything I own to the Lord. You are free to ignore or accept this message, but let me tell you right away, that you are going to be held responsible for the consequences of your decision. As for me, I have taken my decision more than 20 years ago, that as for me and my house, we shall serve the Lord.

The cross is a symbol of crises. It is also a symbol of choice. You have to make a personal choice not to go to hell fire.

The cross is a figure of frustration and adversity. It is a symbol of punishment and suffering. How convenient will you feel, if I ask you to spread your two arms for an hour or two? I am sure you will cry in pain.

The cross typifies suffering and redemption from sin. It addresses the direction which means a lot to man. It goes backward and it addresses the past. It goes forward and addresses the future. It goes inward and addresses our innermost feelings. It goes outwards and points to what we must fight, ignore or come to terms with.

The cross is a horrible instrument of torture. A man who is on the cross goes through a painful death. He dies slowly. Therefore, any man associated with the cross is regarded as a dead man.

Deliverance From Spirit Husband and Spirit Wife

In those days, whenever any man was condemned to death on the cross, members of his family would gather together and begin to cry, because their relative was going to die in a very shameful manner. The cross terminates the transaction with the world. The moment a man is taken out to die on the cross, everyone would begin to cry and wail for him. Some people would even accompany him to the cross knowing that, it was going to be his last day on earth. No matter how sympathetic the crowd may be, it is only the man who actually hangs on the cross who knows the shame, the ridicules and the pains of crucifixion.

The cross is a symbol of life through death, light through darkness, glory through shame and redemption through death.

The cross is the place where God judges sin. There, God took sin and sinful flesh out of the way.

The cross became God's instrument for killing the flesh to die in disgrace and dishonour. Jesus gave us an example. He showed the only way to please the Father - the way of crucifixion. Many love the miracles of Jesus but few are ready to bear the cross of the Lord Jesus. Relatives of those who were nailed to the cross felt miserable. The cross was equivalent to a social stigma.

The cross is the only thing that can siphon the poison of the old serpent out of our lives. Through the cross the venom of the serpent is rendered ineffective. A man who has been to the cross is free from the poison of the serpent. The serpent no longer has any power over him . But for a man who refuses to be crucified, the poison of the old serpent will continue to work in his blood stream. Avoid the cross and keep your satanic poison. Push away the cross and live with the poison of the serpent. The cross is God's strategy of rendering the devil impotent.

The cross was God's instrument for removing the nature of the devil from our lives. The cross is the terminating point of the old Adamic nature.

At the cross, all the sinful habits, sicknesses, disobedience, bad behaviours, evil traits and so on are terminated.

The cross is the gate way to prosperity, wealth, signs, wonders and miracles.

The cross is the power of God. When you get to the cross, all carnal substitutes will fade away. You must take a trip to Golgotha, if you must have power with God and man.

When you are crucified, the world will shout, 'These are the men turning the world upside down.' Of course, this is necessary.

Have you experienced the cross? Have you become a captive of the cross? Have you embraced the message of a shameful death?

Generally the cross is reserved for the worst criminals.

They are usually stripped naked and hanged on the cross. Jesus was numbered with notorious criminals. Can you imagine that the Saviour of the world was naked on the cross, just to pay the price for your salvation? He was put to shame and ridiculed openly. That is why the Bible reveals that the Roman soldier had to cast lots to see who was going to claim Jesus' dress.

Again to hang on the tree was to be reckoned as an accursed person on earth and in heaven. A man who dies on the cross is rejected, as it was both in heaven and on earth. Thus a crucified man is judged as unfit to live either in heaven or on earth.

Let us think about the life of Jesus again. When He was born, angels announced His birth. Great men went to see Him. Throughout His ministry, until He was in the garden of Gethsemane, angels ministered to Him. But the moment He was hanged on the cross, angels deserted Him. The Roman soldiers ridiculed Him, mocked and laughed at Him. There was nobody on His side. The road to the cross was painful and tortuous.

The cross is the point where God's will and your will cross each other. It is the place where you lay down your life for Jesus. Nobody will take your life from you by force, you have to voluntarily lay it down yourself.

Your cross is not a particular problem or sickness. It is that point where you take a decision that you will no longer please yourself. The only people who have genuine authority over Satan are those who choose to die on the cross.

Here is the greatest news of all the ages. It was on the cross that Satan was defeated. It was there that he was.. completely disgraced, and destroyed. If you want to reign, in life therefore, be crucified.

The cross is a throne. If you want to know what it means to exercise power and dominion over satan, you must go to the throne and be crucified. But take note that the moment you decide to die on the cross. Oppositions will arise from everywhere. Decorative people will come from all directions to tell you that the cross is too painful, and shameful. You must turn deaf ears to such deceptive words. Go ahead and crucify the flesh. You must allow the cross to slay the flesh. Do not feel sorry for the flesh. The Bible says, "The flesh profiteth nothing." If you do not kill the flesh, it will kill you. If you do not get rid of the flesh, it will get rid of you.

If you are fond of taking the easy way out of spiritual principles, you are not on the cross. It is possible to choose to remain at the foot of the cross rather than climb up the cross where the crucifixion took place. It is very easy to choose a more convenient place when it comes to crucifixion. Somebody might decide to stay at the foot of the cross while telling himself that it is better to stay there than to move away from the cross. It is clear that the foot of the cross is not the cross.

Deliverance From Spirit Husband and Spirit Wife

A lot of Christians are only abiding at the foot of the cross, they refuse to die on the cross. I always feel nauseated whenever I come across Christians who claim to be so close to God but are living in the flesh.

I went to a Christian bookshop to buy some books. The young man who attended to me called me aside and said that he was going to give me a discount. I thanked him, not knowing that he was trying to play a game. He gave me a receipt and asked me to give him part of the discount he had allowed me, as he needed the money to eat. It was at that point that I realised that he had been cheating on his employer in order to enrich his pocket. Then I asked why he had chosen to work in a Christian organisation and at the same time want to go to hell because of money. He became afraid. That is an example of Christians who are near the cross but are not crucified.

All those who want to live crucified lives and yet live like any other person are deceiving themselves. Can you be talkative and claim to be crucified at the same time? How can you exaggerate and tell white lies and claim that you are crucified? How can you become too intimate with those whom you are not married to? How can you say that the cross is at the centre of your life when you are so self-centred? How can you say that the flesh has been crucified when you get angry at the slightest provocation?

All the pastors who secretly extort money from

innocent members are not crucified. All the pastors who have become professional beggars in the name of preaching are not crucified. Such pastors visit the rich and the privileged. They will never visit poor members. A pastor recently asked me why his church offerings were reducing very fast.

I simply told him to pray believing that the situation would change. He prayed one sunday and decided to give a large offering to God. Out of curiosity he checked up the offering. To his amazement, all the crisp notes which he dropped into the offering bag were nowhere to be found. He quickly summoned the usher in charge of counting the church offerings. The usher was searched and, surprisingly, the money was found in his pocket. But why should that happen in a Pentecostal church? Somebody can listen to every sermon on revival and never get revived. Somebody can pray fervently about having a relationship with God but to no avail.

There are many church members who drink and smoke secretly. There are lots of choir members who have boy-friends and girl-friends. Again there are members who attend worldly parties and do what everyone around is doing, because there are no brothers around to challenge them. Self-display and self-exhortation show that you are not crucified. Gluttony, lust, lack of self-control, hypocrisy and other forms of ungodly attitudes are evidences that you are not crucified.

Deliverance From Spirit Husband and Spirit Wife

There are so-called Christians who are ready to go away from a church that preaches sound doctrine, just because their pet sins are touched.

There are ladies who would run away from living churches just because of cosmetics. They are not crucified. They are living in the valley. Women and men who hear the word of God, but fail to make restitution in the area of marriage has never been to the calvary. Young men and women who steal their parents' money or drive their parents' cars secretly without permission are not crucified.

Many years ago there was a pastor who had a very embarrassing problem. He was bed-wetting. As a result of this he never accepted any invitation to preach outside his station. Somehow he was forced to accept a particular invitation. He preached powerfully and went to sleep. By the time he woke up around 4.00 a.m. he realised that he had wet the bed. Out of shame, he ran to the room of his interpreter asking her to exchange bed .with him so that his host would believe that it was the sister-interpreter who wet the bed. What was his problem? He was not crucified.

If something happens to you and you lock up your door and cry out of self-pity you are not crucified.

If you give in to resentment and malice, you are not crucified.

When you refuse to accept blame for your wrong doing

you have not been to the cross.

If you are quick to shift blame and not ready to take responsibility for anything, you have never known the cross of Christ.

When you take offence at everything people say to you, you have not been to the cross.

The truth, beloved, is that very few Christians are living the crucified life. That is why the power of God is disappearing fast from many churches, and prayer meetings have become formalities.

The only parts of our nature which the devil can never touch are those parts which have been crucified. The only time that Satan cannot touch the believer is when he is on the cross.

If your thoughts, your handling of money, your sexual life, your temper, and your eating habits are not crucified, then you have not started at all, because the devil can easily manipulate you. The devil will always triumph over a believer who is not on the cross.

The cross is the only place of safety. It is the only place where we have power. Without the cross, you are susceptible to all forms of satanic attack.

Lack of crucifixion can prevent the fullness of the Holy Spirit from being manifested in our lives. The crucifixion must start from the innermost part. We must say bye-bye to worldly ambitions and the pride of life. We must be ready to part with friends who are enemies of God.

Deliverance From Spirit Husband and Spirit Wife

Spiritual arrogance must go. Your past religious experiences must be sacrificed at the cross. Worldly gains, worldly preferences, the praise of men and fleshly comfort, must be crucified.

Jesus went to the cross and was crucified, to show us that the cross is unavoidable. By going to the cross He showed us that crucifixion is possible. To reject the cross is to reject everything that is for your utmost good.

The cross divides men into two categories. Those who are earthly-bound and those whom heaven is their goal. Those who get irritably offended and refuse to forgive those who offend them and those who are envious, are not on the cross.

It is possible for a man to give up a lucrative profession, in order to make more money in the ministry. Such a person is living in self-deceits. The service will be worthless. If you are working for God, and you are seeking for power just to make a name for yourself, you are not crucified

The flesh was defeated by Christ, legally, at the cross. If you want to experience legal and practical victory over the flesh, then you must be crucified with Jesus. How can we do this? The Bible says:

What shall we say then? Shall we continue in sin, that grace may abound? God forbid. How shall we, that are dead to sin, live any longer therein? Know ye not, that so many of us as were baptized into Jesus Christ were baptized into his death? Therefore we are buried with him by baptism into death: that like

Deliverance From Spirit Husband and Spirit Wife

as Christ was raised up from the dead by the glory of the Father, even so we also should walk in newness of life. For if we have been planted together in the likeness of his death, we shall be also in the likeness of his resurrection: Knowing this, that our old man is crucified with him, that the body of sin might be destroyed, that henceforth we should not serve sin (Romans 6:1-6).

What can we gain from this Scripture?

Firstly, recognise the fact that sin has been defeated for you, hence, sin has no right to control you. Verse 7 tells us another important thing, "For he that is dead is freed from sin." What do we learn from this? A dead man does not commit fornication, does not get angry, or steal. A dead man does not abuse or fight with people.

Again verse 8 tells us, "If we be dead with Christ we believe that we shall also live with him" This simply means that if the flesh is not dead you will not be able to reign with Christ when the time comes.

Secondly, reckon yourself dead unto sin but alive unto God. For example, if somebody often gets angry and he wants to reckon himself dead to anger, he should simply refuse to do what he normally does each time he gets angry. The demon of anger loves expression. To reckon yourself dead unto anger, you must refuse to allow it to express itself.

Again if your problem has been malice and unforgiving spirit, what do you do? If the devil tells you not to greet a particular person, if you want to reckon yourself dead to malice, you will simply walk up to him or her and greet the person. You may even decide to buy a gift for somebody you attempted to keep malice with.

I remember the story of a brother who died and was kept in the mortuary, awaiting burial. After four days, the mortuary attendant found tears on his face. It was a strange sight. He woke up from the death bed after four days. After he rose up, he could not eat. Eventually, he opened his mouth and began to declare what he saw when he died. He made a particular startling statement. According to him, there is a particular department in heaven where there is an angel. All that the angel did was ask for your name and all the sins you ever committed (for which you never asked for forgiveness or covered the same with the blood of Jesus) would appear on a large screen.

He narrated the story of a particular man who stood before that angel. The angel asked the man, "Do you say that you are a Christian?" "Yes", the man replied. The angel said, "But what is this in your pockets? The man dipped his hand into his pocket and brought out anger and pride. The angel asked him, "But why did you allow these sins in your life?" "The devil deceived me", said the man. The angel asked him to wait while he summoned the devil. The brother said that he was so surprised that instead of an ugly looking creature, it was a handsome person who came forward as the devil. He was asked why he deceived the man. He laughed and said, "Mr. man, can you tell me the kind of clothing I was wearing, the day I came to deceive you?" The man could not answer the question. The devil laughed again and dragged the man into hell fire.

Finally, let us look at the third key. Agree to suffer or lose your position instead of committing sin. To say 'No', is the best thing to do rather than to compromise.

A Christian travelled abroad for further studies and decided to stay on in the country. The only option he had to remain a legal immigrant was to take up a white lady as a wife in a kind of marriage of convenience. The Christian brother felt reluctant initially. He had lots of pressure which made him to eventually find one white lady who agreed to go into a mock-marriage with him for a little money.

This born again Christian thought that he was being smart. On the particular day he was supposed to obtain his residence permit based on the fact that he had married a white lady, the lady called him and told him that she would go back on the agreement, unless the so-called Christian brother was ready to act as a real husband to her. The brother was surprised, and confused. He contacted a minister who told him that it did not matter and that he was free to have sex with the woman since that was the only way to collect his residence permit. He was misguided. He carried out the instruction, committed the sin with the woman and contacted AIDS. That was how he became a candidate of hell fire. A Christian who has been to the cross will not do that.

THE CROSS OR THE WAY OF THE CROSS

It has become increasingly difficult to come across Bible-based messages these days. A lot of ministers major in the goodies of the gospel. They remove every thing pertaining to the cross from their messages. They, rather, prefer smooth sermons and other things that entertain their hearers and relegate the message of the cross to the background. If you desire to hear the type of sermon that Jesus preached, you have to look very far before you can find the preacher who has both the message and the mind of Christ. That is how far the situation has degenerated into, and this should make us weep!

There is no other pathway to the heavenly city except through the way of the cross.

We cannot become fervent spiritually except we go back to the cross. No cross, no fire.

To avoid the way of the cross is to remain cold spiritually. Many people are looking for Jesus where miracles are taking place. You can only find Jesus at the cross. He resides at the cross. You will never know what it means to be hot spiritually, and burn with Holy Ghost fire, until you surrender all you have at the foot of the cross. Beloved, the problem we have today is that the cross has been forgotten and the flesh has been enthroned.

The greatest tragedy that mankind has ever known is the error of putting the flesh on the throne and celebrating the coronation of man's untamed nature. What happens when Mr. Flesh is on the throne? Your guess is as good as mine. But let us go beyond what we can guess as human beings. How does God look at those who deliberately decide to worship the flesh? How does He view those who are bent on doing what they like and pleasing the dictates of the flesh?

The word of God makes it clear that the flesh is totally useless in the sight of God. No amount of white-washing would make it acceptable to God. The Bible says,

If any man would come after me, let him deny himself, let him carry his cross daily and follow after me (Luke 9:23).

This passage tells us, clearly, that without the cross there is no Christianity.

There is no possibility of living the Christian life that is approved before the Almighty without carrying your cross. For you to continue to experience abundant life, you must first, carry your cross, deny yourself and follow Jesus. You must do this daily, and follow Jesus all the way.

In a nutshell, to deny yourself means to say no to your flesh whenever it demands for carnal pleasures, sinful actions, and when all forms of things that violate God's word raise their ugly heads, you say no.

Deliverance From Spirit Husband and Spirit Wife

We must echo the prayer of Jesus in the garden of Gethsemane when He said, "Not my will, but Thy will be done." But how many of us are ready to say that today? It is easy to say that we have given our lives to Christ, but the qualities of our decision will be revealed at the time of trial. We can ascertain if you have truly surrendered your WILL to God only when you come face to face with the practical life situations. What will you do if you have to make a choice between doing the will of God and getting financial gain? Won't you opt for financial gain?

I remember a sister who claimed that she had surrendered her will to God, and went ahead to pray that God should reveal to her to whom to get married. God showed her in a vision, a brother who was blind in one eye. Immediately she woke up, she began to argue and cancel the vision, saying that God could never have revealed the one-eyed man to her as her future husband. She prayed telling God the kind of man she would like to marry.

That shows that she was only ready to do her own will and not the will of God. Yet, those who want to deny themselves and take up their cross, will simply say, "Lord as a human being, I would not make my choice I am ready to do your will. You know what is best for me. Thy will be done." It is only after you have denied yourself, that you can go ahead to take up your cross and follow Jesus. A man who is truly ready to deny himself would neither be ashamed of taking up the cross nor reluctant to do so.

A cross is not beautiful to behold. It is not fashionable, rather it is old-fashioned. The cross of Jesus is the old-fashioned cross. One song writer has described it as, "The old rugged cross."

What is the cross? The cross is the place where God's will crosses yours. We can then say that we are carrying our cross, when we drop our own will and lift up the will of God as our only choice. To accept the cross is to decide to align yourself with the will of God. The cross is a place of execution.

In the sixth book of Romans verse 6, we are told that, "our old man is crucified with Him." What the Bible is saying is that, the rebellious, sinful nature, which we inherited from Adam must be dealt with through crucifixion.

That is God's only solution for the flesh. Without crucifixion the problem of the flesh cannot be solved. Deliverance does not remove the problem of the flesh. If you go through deliverance a thousand and one times, but fail to deal with your flesh and your carnal nature, you will always have spiritual problems. You cannot cast out the flesh. You can only cast out evil spirit.

A lot of people think that they can bribe God by going through deliverance. Those who fall into terrible sins and keep on running to attend deliverance programmes without taking a sober look at their lives, and dealing a decisive blow on the flesh, are only wasting their time. The only scriptural method for dealing with the flesh is to crucify it. God does not send Mr. Flesh to the Sunday school or the Bible college; neither does He send the flesh to a seminar, on "How to improve your self-image."

God's solution to the nagging problems of the flesh is simple and final-execution. The flesh must be given a mortal blow.

The good news of the gospel, is that the execution of the flesh took place some 2000 years ago, when Jesus was on the cross. Our old man was crucified with Him. It is a historical fact.

More than that, it is a spiritual fact. It is true, whether we believe it or not. The only thing is that we cannot benefit from it until we come into practical terms with the call to crucifixion. The flesh detests crucifixion, yet it has to be crucified.

God has made three provisions to rescue man from the grip of sin and the flesh.

One, He has to deal with our sins- all the sinful acts which we have carried out.

Two, He has to deal with the corrupt nature - that thing in us which makes us to go on committing sin.

Three, God has to replace our old man with a new one.

So we can see that God's solution for delivering us from the powers and shackles of sin, is to deal with our total spiritual needs. This is where people get stuck.

How does God deal with our sin?

Through forgiveness. When you commit a sin, He forgives you. However, if He shows you what is bad and you stubbornly go ahead to do it, with the decision that you are ready to ignore the consequence, then there is no repentance and there is no forgiveness. You will receive your stripes complete from God. You knew that it was wrong and you went ahead to do evil. But for the things you do ignorantly and you are truly repentant of, you will be forgiven.

God has to deal with our corrupt nature which cause us to commit sin. God's provision for this problem is for you to allow him to put the sinful nature to death. How then will God replace the old man with the new man? How will God give you a heart transplant? The Bible says, "Ye put off concerning the former conversation, the old man which is corrupt according to the deceitful lust and be renewed in the spirit of your mind. And that Ye put on the new man which after God is created in righteousness and true holiness."

There is no short-cut to receiving the power of God. You must put off the old man and put on the new man. When that takes place in your life, people will notice glaring changes. You will become a brand-new man or woman. Until your friends and acquaintances notice the change in your life, you cannot claim that you have had an encounter with Christ. When you have an encounter with Christ, unbelievers will either complain about or commend your life.

Beloved, do not assume that the old man will passively accept crucifixion. The flesh will not accept the sentence of execution without argument. On the contrary, the flesh will struggle, fight, kick and rebel against any attempt to get it executed. That is why Apostle Paul warned in Galatians 3:3 that you must put the flesh to death, so that it does not regain control over you. It will always struggle to gain control over you. Many Christians do not understand the divine provision. They have therefore kept deliverance ministers busy. They claim that their sins have been forgiven only to go back to those sins, running an evil circle. Today, they are forgiven, tomorrow they commit another sin. Such a life style leaves much to be desired. They are yet to experience freedom from the power of the fallen human nature.

A lot of people go about saying that they are sanctified. But how can a sanctified man make his wife a punching bag? How can those who say they are holy, be the same group of people who tell lies, steal money and fight with everyone around? Sanctified indeed! Sometimes the so-called sanctified man comes back to say, "Sorry, I have lost my sanctification. How can I regain it?" That is not the question. You should arrange to execute the old man. Why do not you look inward at this moment and take a personal inventory, to ascertain your standing with God?

Are you completely free from the shackles of the flesh? Are you completely free from the domination of Mr. Flesh?

Can you say that you now put on the new man? Can you personally echo the word of an old song writer: "The thing I used to do I do them no more?"

The death of the flesh makes it impossible for the works of the flesh to operate in our lives as witchcraft.

CHAPTER NINE

Prayer Section

Prayer is a gift to you and a privilege. The gift is offered to all and all may become the wielders of the great power in prayer. However, the fact remains that the power of prayer is least exercised by the average believer. You will do well to learn the art of warfare prayer. The present temperature of the prayer of many Christians needs to rise if they expect serious breakthroughs.

The prayer points in this section are targeted at confronting and defeating spirit wives and spirit husbands. This is how to use the prayer points:

1. Go about the prayers in any of the following ways as led by the Holy Spirit:

   a. Three days' night vigil, i.e. praying from 10:00 P.M. to 5:00 A.M. three-consecutive nights.

   b. Three days' fast (breaking daily), i.e. praying at intervals and breaking the fast at 6.00 P.M. or 9.00.P.M. daily.

   c. Seven days' night vigil, i.e. praying from 10:00 P.M.

to 5:00 A.M. seven-consecutive nights.

d. Seven days' fast (breaking daily), i.e. praying at intervals and breaking the fast at 6.00 P.M. or 9.00.P.M. daily.

e. Three or more days of dry fast., i.e. praying and fasting three or more days without any food or drink.

2. Pray aggressively.

NOTE: Spend part of the vigil or fasting praying in the Spirit - Praying in the spirit is the ability to pray in tongues as given utterance by the Holy Spirit. To pray in the Spirit, you must have been baptised in the Holy Ghost (not water baptism) - 1Cor. 14:15.

You will be victorious, in Jesus' name.

1. PERSONAL DELIVERANCE FROM SPIRITUAL MARRIAGES

When you understand self-deliverance, you will keep yourself from being demonised; you will keep yourself healthy, physically and spiritually and be free from demonic pollution. Every day, you will enjoy divine health and will not be spending your money on drugs and hospital bills.

Sometimes, there may be no minister who is anointed and knowledgeable about deliverance to help you. Sometimes, you can be heavily attacked in your dream and the next service is about four days away. What do you do? You should never allow evil spirits to reside in your life. If you lack adequate time to do a self-deliverance in the mornings, after your quiet time, then, when you're having your bath, you could do it.

Our environment is such that there are many evil spirits moving around and if you are not regularly cleaning your house, they may lodge there; your level of education notwithstanding. If a university professor could carry a ritual sacrifice because he needed promotion, then education is irrelevant.

Let's learn a few lessons now before we go into the actual practice.

A demon is a spirit, which means it's like a wind or breath. Most evil spirits leave through the breathing passage or by any opening in the body. This is why sometimes when prayers are hot some people begin to pass out gas or emit bad odours. Now, when an ambulance goes through a busy area, it blares its siren. The purpose is to clear the traffic so as to expedite its passage.

Therefore, after praying for self-deliverance, you should keep quiet before ejecting those evil spirits. This is why at times we ask people to breath in and out. If you are praying or speaking at this time, the spirits will not go out because you have not opened the way for them.

The next lesson you must learn is this: demons can come out by simple breathing, coughing, choking, yawning, vomiting, etc. The manifestations vary according to the person and the spirits involved. All the spirits that are not deeply rooted, depart easily, but those deeply entrenched, will require more time and effort to be made to go. The more stubborn ones will require the help of other believers. However, even when they are that strong, and you continue to wound them daily, they will eventually be mortally wounded.

Also, know that if multiple spirits are responsible for one problem, all of them must be removed before total victory is assured. One thing is certain; with every inch of ground grabbed from the devil, you will notice a definite improvement in your life. This is certain. Once the spirit leaves you, there will be a change in you.

Also, remember that an evil spirit must have a legal ground for staying in a person's life.

Deliverance From Spirit Husband and Spirit Wife

The purpose of all this information is to enable you to do a self-deliverance at home for yourself.

The process of self-deliverance is carried out in stages. Let's go through them one by one.

Step ONE

Start with praise worship. You can sing songs to praise God or worship Him.

Step TWO

Confess out loud scriptures promising deliverance. Let us run through a few of them: Luke 10:19, Ephesians 1:7, Romans 16:20, Revelation 12:11, Colossians 2:14,15, Galatians 3:13,14, Psalm 91:3, and 2 Tim. 4:18. You must memorise at least 2 Tim. 4:18 which says:

And the Lord shall deliver me from every evil work, and will preserve me unto His heavenly kingdom: to whom be glory for ever and ever. Amen.

Step THREE

Break covenants and curses to destroy their legal hold. You pray a simple prayer: "I break any curse or covenant linking me with spirit wife / spirit husband." This is a simple prayer with much result.

Step FOUR

Bind all the spirits associated with those covenants

and curses like this: "I bind all the spirits attached or connected to the curses and covenants I have just broken, in the name of Jesus."

Step FIVE

Lay one hand on your head and the other on your stomach or navel and begin to pray like this: "Holy Ghost fire, burn from the top of my head to the sole of my feet." Begin to mention every organ of your body: your kidney, liver, intestine, blood, etc. You must not rush at this level. Lay your hands on areas that the Spirit of God leads you to. Do not be afraid if you notice that you are swaying or staggering, etc.

Step SIX

Then saturate yourself with the blood of Jesus. You do this by saying: "Blood of Jesus, enter into my spirit, soul and body." Next you say: "I drink the blood of Jesus." This must continue until you have a release in your spirit to stop.

Step SEVEN

It is now that you are able to demand firmly in the name of the Lord Jesus Christ, that any spirit that is not of God should leave you. You demand it forcefully like this: "In the name of the Lord Jesus Christ, I come against all you hidden spirits and I bind your activities in my life. You can no longer hide below the surface because I now recognise what you have been doing; release me, in the name of Jesus." "You spirit husband/wife, I speak to you directly, get out of my life now. I am redeemed by the blood of Jesus Christ, come out and go now. Go out with every breath by the power of the Holy Spirit. I prevail over you."

Then you stop talking; open your mouth and nose and begin to breath in and out. Take about three to seven deep breaths, and expel them forcefully through your mouth and nose. You may be surprised that strange things will begin to happen. Repeat this again and again. This will help you to flush out any evil deposit or impurity in your body. You may notice that you are coughing, yawning, sneezing, sweating or shedding tears, but continue and do not lose your concentration.

Step EIGHT

When you have finished the expulsion stage, you then ask for a fresh in-filling of the Holy Spirit. And close the session with praises.

When you are attacked in your dream, rise up and go through the stages I have already mentioned. You can also pray the prayer points on victory over satanic dreams at the end of this book.

Self-deliverance keeps you from getting sick; it removes every evil seed of the enemy; it charges your body with fire. It uproots evil plantations and builds up your confidence.

Every night before you go to bed, you must remember these three important prayer points.

1. Pray that the walls of fire should surround you. The Bible says:

For I, saith the Lord, will be unto her a wall of fire round about, and will be the glory in the midst of her (Zec. 2:5).

2. Pray for cover with the blood of Jesus.

And they overcame him by the blood of the Lamb, and by the word of their testimony; and they loved not their lives unto the death (Rev 12:11).

3. Also pray that the angels of God should surround you.

The angel of the LORD encampeth round about them that fear him, and delivereth them (Ps 34:7).

No matter how sleepy you are, make sure you pray these three prayer points nightly.

There is no reason self-deliverance should not be effective. However, if the person seeking deliverance is under stubborn demonic control or hereditary strongman and lacks sufficient faith or authority to defeat the oppressors or if he is living in any known sin, the evil spirits will defend what they think is their right.

One final word of caution. For a person to be delivered, he must want deliverance. Self deliverance must not be done because of pride, shyness, the fear of possible public embarrassment, etc. Your motive for engaging in it has to be pure.

Deliverance From Spirit Husband and Spirit Wife

Remember, deliverance is a process and the length of time it takes depends on several things viz: the length of time the spirit has stayed inside a person, the strength and reinforcement of the spirit, the experience and degree of anointing upon those who are ministering the deliverance, the willingness of the person being delivered to be free, the knowledge of the word of God and your level of hatred for sin.

For self-deliverance to be very effective, a great deal of self-discipline is necessary.

Also, remember that bondage can be weak or strong. A weak hold can be broken quickly, whereas a stronghold may take a longer time. You will not realise the strength of a bondage until you faithfully and persistently work on it. You must remember that a foothold can graduate to a stronghold if left unaddressed.

---

2. POWER AGAINST EVIL SPIRITUAL MARRIAGES

Praise worship

Confession

1. Spirit husband/spirit wife, release me by fire, in the name of Jesus.
2. Every spirit husband/wife, I divorce you by the blood of Jesus.
3. Every spirit wife/every spirit husband, die, in the name

Deliverance From Spirit Husband and Spirit Wife

of Jesus.

4. Everything you have deposited in my life, come out by fire, in the name of Jesus.

5. Every power that is working against my marriage, fall down and die, in the name of Jesus.

6. I divorce and renounce my marriage with the spirit husband or wife, in the name of Jesus.

7. I break all covenants entered into with the spirit husband or wife, in the name of Jesus.

8. I command the thunder fire of God to burn to ashes the wedding gown, ring, photographs and all other materials used for the marriage, in Jesus' name.

9. I send the fire of God to burn to ashes the marriage certificate, in the name of Jesus.

10. I break every blood and soul-tie covenants with the spirit husband or wife, in the name of Jesus.

11. I send thunder fire of God to burn to ashes the children born to the marriage, in Jesus' name.

12. I withdraw my blood, sperm or any other part of my body deposited in the altar of the spirit husband or wife, in the name of Jesus.

13. You spirit husband or wife tormenting my life and earthly marriage I bind you with hot chains and fetters of God and cast you out of my life into the deep pit, and I command you not to ever come into my life again, in the name of Jesus.

14. I return to you every property of yours in my possession in the spirit world, including the dowry and whatsoever

Deliverance From Spirit Husband and Spirit Wife

was used for the marriage and covenants, in the name of Jesus.

15. I drain myself of all evil materials deposited in my body as a result of our sexual relation, in Jesus' name

16. Lord, send Holy Ghost fire into my root and burn out all unclean things deposited in it by the spirit husband or wife, in the name of Jesus.

17. I break the head of the snake deposited into my body by the spirit husband or wife to do me harm, and command it to come out, in the name of Jesus.

18. I purge out, with the blood of Jesus, every evil material deposited in my womb to prevent me from having children on earth.

19. Lord, repair and restore every damage done to any part of my body and my earthly marriage by the spirit husband or wife, in the name of Jesus.

20. I reject and cancel every curse, evil pronouncement, spell, jinx, enchantment and incantation placed upon me by the spirit husband or wife, in the name of Jesus.

21. I take back and possess all my earthly belongings in the custody of the spirit husband or wife, in Jesus' name.

22. I command the spirit husband or wife to turn his or her back on me forever, in Jesus' name.

23. I renounce and reject the name given to me by the spirit husband or wife, in the name of Jesus.

24. I hereby declare and confess that the Lord Jesus Christ is my Husband for eternity, in Jesus' name.

25. I soak myself in the blood of Jesus and cancel the evil

Deliverance From Spirit Husband and Spirit Wife

mark or writings placed on me, in Jesus' name.

26. I set myself free from the stronghold and domineering power and bondage of the spirit husband or wife, in the name of Jesus.

27. I paralyse the remote control power and work used to destabilise my earthly marriage and to hinder me from bearing children for my earthly husband or wife, in the name of Jesus.

28. I announce to the heavens that I am married forever to Jesus.

29. Every trademark of evil marriage, be shaken out of my life, in the name of Jesus.

30. Every evil writing engraved by iron pen, be wiped off by the blood of Jesus.

31. I bring the blood of Jesus upon the spirit that does not want to go, in the name of Jesus.

32. I bring the blood of Jesus on every evidence that can be tendered by wicked spirit against me.

33. I file a counter-report in the heavens against every evil marriage, in the name of Jesus.

34. I refuse to supply any evidence that the enemy may use against me, in the name of Jesus.

35. Let satanic exhibitions be destroyed by the blood of Jesus.

36. I declare to you spirit wife / husband that there is no vacancy for you in my life, in the name of Jesus.

37. O Lord, make me a vehicle of deliverance.

38. I come by faith to mount Zion. Lord, command

Deliverance From Spirit Husband and Spirit Wife

deliverance upon my life now.

39. Lord, water me from the waters of God.

40. Let the careful siege of the enemy be dismantled, in the name of Jesus.

41. O Lord, defend Your interest in my life.

42. Everything written against me in the cycle of the moon against me, be blotted out, in Jesus' name.

43. Everything programmed into the sun, moon and stars against me, be dismantled, in Jesus' name.

44. Every evil thing programmed into my genes, be blotted out by the blood of Jesus.

45. O Lord, shake out seasons of failure and frustrations from my life.

46. I overthrow every wicked law working against my life, in the name of Jesus.

47. I ordain a new time, season and profitable law, in the name of Jesus.

48. I speak destruction unto the palaces of the queen of the coast and of the rivers, in Jesus' name.

49. I speak destruction unto the headquarters of the spirit of Egypt and blow up their altars, in the name of Jesus.

50. I speak destruction unto the altars speaking against the purpose of God for my life, in Jesus' name.

51. I declare myself a virgin for the Lord, in Jesus' name

52. Let every evil veil upon my life be torn open, in the name of Jesus.

53. Every wall between me and the visitation of God, be broken, in the name of Jesus.

54. Let the counsel of God prosper in my life, in the name of Jesus.
55. I destroy the power of any demonic seed in my life from the womb, in the name of Jesus.
56. I speak unto my umbilical gate to overthrow all negative parental spirits, in the name of Jesus.
57. I break the yoke of the spirits having access to my reproductive gates, in the name of Jesus.
58. O Lord, let Your time of refreshing come upon me.
59. I bring fire from the altar of the Lord upon every evil marriage, in the name of Jesus.
60. I redeem myself by the blood of Jesus from every sex trap, in the name of Jesus.
61. I erase the engraving of my name on any evil marriage record, in the name of Jesus.
62. I reject and renounce every evil spiritual marriage, in the name of Jesus.
63. I confess that Jesus is my original spouse and is jealous over me.
64. I issue a bill of divorcement to every spirit wife / husband, in the name of Jesus.
65. I bind every spirit wife / husband with everlasting chains, in the name of Jesus.
66. Let heavenly testimony overcome every evil testimony of hell, in the name of Jesus.
67. O Lord, bring to my remembrance every spiritual trap and contract.
68. Let the blood of Jesus purge me of every contaminating

material, in the name of Jesus.

69. Let the spirit husband/wife fall down and die, in the name of Jesus.

70. Let all your children attached to me fall down and die, in the name of Jesus.

71. I burn your certificates and destroy your rings, in the name of Jesus.

72. I execute judgement against water spirits and I declare that you are reserved for everlasting chains in darkness, in the name of Jesus.

73. O Lord, contend with those who are contending with me.

74. Every trademark of water spirit, be shaken out of my life, in the name of Jesus.

---

3. DEALING WITH SPIRITUAL ARMED ROBBERS

Praise worship

Confession

1. You messenger of death, come out by fire, in the name of Jesus.

(Lay your right hand on your head as you take this prayer point aggressively)

2. Every arrow of death and destruction, go back to your sender, in the name of Jesus.

3. You spirit husband / wife and caterers, die, in the name of Jesus.

244

Deliverance From Spirit Husband and Spirit Wife

4. I reject every plan of the enemy to weaken my spiritual life, in the name of Jesus.

5. Every spirit coming to defile my soul and body, I break your backbone today, in the name of Jesus.

6. Listen to me, you spirit wive and spirit husband. I am married to Jesus. Depart from my life by fire, in the name of Jesus.

7. You spirit husband/wive, I reject every token of marriage that you are holding onto in my life, in Jesus' name.

8. Let the fire of God come down and burn these evil tokens to ashes, in the name of Jesus.

9. O earth, hear the word of the Lord. Swallow every spiritual rapist targeted against me, in Jesus' name.

10. You spirit wive/husband, I command the thunder of God to blind your eyes and you will no longer see me, in the name of Jesus.

11. Every spirit of witchcraft manifesting in the form of dog or serpent, I resist you, in the name of Jesus.

12. Every spiritual intercourse material deposited in me by evil spiritual partner, come out of my body, in the name of Jesus.

13. Every spirit oppressing me in my dream, I declare my house a danger zone for you, in Jesus' name.

14. I destroy every sexual blood covenant operating against my life, in the name of Jesus.

15. I break every sexual soul-tie arising from old relationship, in the name of Jesus.

16. I destroy the power of sexual remote control working

against my life, in the name of Jesus.

17. I break every sexual curse upon my life, in Jesus' name.

18. Every evil spiritual children, fall down and die, in the name of Jesus.

19. Every satanic spiritual marital home, I set you ablaze by the fire of the Holy Spirit, in the name of Jesus.

20. Any material from my body present in any satanic bank and used to oppress me spiritually, I retrieve you by the blood of Jesus.

21. Every spirit of seduction working against my life, physically or spiritually, I bind you and cast you out, in the name of Jesus.

22. I release my reproductive organ from any demonic control or possession, in the name of Jesus.

23. Every spiritual contamination of my physical marital sexual relationship, I sanitise you by the blood of Jesus.

24. I destroy every knowledge and memory of any evil sexual book or literature that I have ever read, in the name of Jesus.

25. I command the following spirits to come out of my life and release me, in the name of Jesus.

- masturbation	- pornography
- homosexuality	- lust of the eyes
- sexual perversion	- oral sex
- anal sex	- bestiality
- incest	- rape
- fornication	- adultery
- immorality	- occultic sex

Deliverance From Spirit Husband and Spirit Wife

- prostitution
- uncleanness
- filthy dreams
- filthy imaginations
- lasciviousness
- promiscuity
- seduction

- harlotry
- filth
- filthy conversations
- sexual flashbacks
- nudity
- flirting
- lust of the flesh

4. FREEDOM FROM INORDINATE AFFECTIONS (Gal. 5:24)

Some people who state that nobody can be free from willful sin or ties with demonic world, are ignorant of God's provision to set man free, and make him free indeed. Appropriate this provision for your life today by ensuring that you crucify your flesh with all its affections and lusts. 1 Cor. 6:16 says,

What? know ye not that he which is joined to an harlot is one body? for two, saith he shall be one flesh.

A soul-tie is an obsessive affection for a person, which is often strengthened by sexual intercourse or blood covenants. When there is soul-tie one's actions are controlled and subject to those of the other person. An unholy union is formed with this person and is consecrated so that the two share minds, purpose and life. One is living for the other person.

A soul-tie can be between a man and a woman; a mother and a son (this is called Olympus complex), a boyfriend and a girlfriend. When a man or woman is manipulated or controlled in the name of love, this bond has to be broken because as far as God is concerned, this is witchcraft.

CONFESSION

Gal 6:17: From henceforth let no man trouble me: for I bear in my body the marks of the Lord Jesus.

PRAISE WORSHIP

1.Thank the Lord for His redemptive power.

2.Prayers of confession of sins and forgiveness.

3.I release myself from all unprofitable friendships, in the name of Jesus.

4.I come against the dark powers which have manipulated my friendship with . . . (*mention the name of the person*) and I break their powers over my life, in the name of Jesus.

5.I bind all demonic authorities which motivated and controlled my relationship with . . . (*mention the name of the person*) and break their authority and power over my affections, in the name of Jesus.

6.I command all evil remote controllers to loose their hold upon my affections, in the name of Jesus.

7.I release myself from the hold of every bewitched relationship, in the name of Jesus.

8.By the blood of Jesus, I remove myself from any strange authority ever exercised over me.

9.I remove all evil soul-ties and affections, in the name of Jesus.

10.I come against every desire and expectation of the enemy to engage me in any unprofitable relationship, in the name of Jesus.

11.I break every ungodly relationship, in Jesus' name.

12. I break and renounce evil soul-tie I have had or may have had with

- secret societies   - cults
- adulterers   - family members
- close friends   - organisations

- husbands	- acquaintances
- wives	- engagements
- doctors	- clubs
- religious leaders	- social organisations
- past or present friends	- preachers, etc.,

in the name of Jesus.

13. I renounce all hidden evil soul-ties, in Jesus' name.

14. I renounce, break and loose myself from all demonic subjection to any relationship, in the name of Jesus.

15. I break all evil soul-ties and wash them away with the blood of the Lord Jesus.

16. I remove myself from any strange authority exercised over me, in the name of Jesus.

17. I remove all mind controlling manipulations between me and any friend or family member, in Jesus' name.

18. I claim deliverance from any negative affection towards anyone, in the name of Jesus.

19. Let evil affections towards me be wiped off the mind of . . . (*mention the name of the person*), in the name of Jesus.

20. Lord Jesus, I give You my affections, emotions and desires and I request that they be in submission to the Holy Spirit.

21. Praise the Lord for answered prayer.

5. VICTORY OVER SATANIC DREAMS

Praise worship

Confession

1. I claim all the good things which God has revealed to me through dreams. I reject all bad and satanic dreams, in the name of Jesus.

2. (You are going to be specific here. Place your hand on your chest and talk to God specifically about the dreams which need to be cancelled. Cancel it with all your strength. If it needs fire, command the fire of God to burn it to ashes.)

3. O Lord, perform the necessary surgical operation in my life and change all that had gone wrong in the spirit world.

4. I claim back all the good things which I have lost as a result of defeat and attacks in my dreams, in the name of Jesus.

5. I arrest every spiritual attacker and paralyse their activities in my life, in the name of Jesus.

6. I retrieve my stolen virtues, goodness and blessings, in the name of Jesus.

7. Let all satanic manipulations through dreams be dissolved, in the name of Jesus.

8. Let all arrows, gunshots, wounds, harassment, opposition in dreams return to the sender, in the name of Jesus.

9. I reject every evil spiritual load placed on me through dreams, in the name of Jesus.

10. All spiritual animals (cats, dogs, snakes, crocodiles) paraded against me, be chained and return to your senders, in the name of Jesus.

11. Holy Ghost, purge my intestine and my blood from satanic foods and injections, in Jesus' name.

12. I break every evil covenant and initiation through dreams, in the name of Jesus.

13. I disband all the hosts of darkness set against me, in the name of Jesus.

14. Every evil imagination and plan contrary to my life, fail woefully, in the name of Jesus.

15. Every doorway and ladder to satanic invasion in my life, be abolished forever by the blood of Jesus.

16. I loose myself from curses, hexes, spells, bewitchment and evil domination directed against me through dreams, in the name of Jesus.

17. I command you ungodly powers to release me, in the name of Jesus.

18. Let all past satanic defeats in the dream be converted to victory, in the name of Jesus.

19. Let all tests in the dream be converted to testimonies, in the name of Jesus.

20. Let all trials in the dream be converted to triumphs, in the name of Jesus.

21. Let all failures in the dream be converted to success, in the name of Jesus.

22. Let all scars in the dream be converted to stars, in the name of Jesus.

23. Let all bondage in the dream be converted to freedom, in the name of Jesus.
24. Let all losses in the dream be converted to gains, in the name of Jesus.
25. Let all opposition in the dream be converted to victory, in the name of Jesus.
26. Let all weaknesses in the dream be converted to strength, in the name of Jesus.
27. Let all negative in the dream be converted to positive, in the name of Jesus.
28. I release myself from every infirmity introduced into my life through dreams, in the name of Jesus.
29. Let all attempts by the enemy to deceive me through dreams fail woefully, in Jesus' name.
30. I reject evil spiritual husband, wife, children, marriage, engagement, trading, pursuit, ornament, money, friend, relative, etc. in the name of Jesus.
31. Lord Jesus, wash my spiritual eyes, ears and mouth with Your blood.
32. The God who answereth by fire should answer by fire whenever any spiritual attacker comes against me.
33. Lord Jesus, replace all satanic dreams with heavenly visions and divinely-inspired dreams.
35. Confess these scriptures out loud: Psalm 27:1-2, 1 Cor. 10:21, Psalm 91.
36. I command every evil plantation in my life: Come out with all your roots, in the name of Jesus! *(Lay your hands on your stomach and keep repeating the*

emphasised area.)

37. Evil strangers in my body, come out of your hiding places, in the name of Jesus. ⁻

38. I disconnect any conscious or unconscious linkage with demonic caterers, in the name of Jesus.

39. Let all avenues of eating or drinking spiritual poisons be closed, in the name of Jesus.

40. I cough out and vomit any food eaten from the table of the devil in the name of Jesus. (*Cough them out and vomit them in faith. Prime the expulsion*).

41. Let all negative materials circulating in my blood stream be evacuated, in the name of Jesus.

42. I drink the blood of Jesus. (*Physically drink and swallow it in faith. Keep doing this for some time*).

43. Let all evil spiritual feeders warring against me drink their own blood and eat their own flesh, in Jesus' name.

44. I command all demonic food utensils fashioned against me to be roasted, in the name of Jesus.

45. Holy Ghost fire, circulate all over my body, in the name of Jesus.

46. I command all physical poisons inside my system to be neutralised, in the name of Jesus.

47. Let all evil assignments fashioned against me through the mouth be nullified, in Jesus' name.

48. Let all spiritual problems attached to any hour of the night be cancelled, in the name of Jesus. (*Pick the periods from midnight to 6:00 a.m.*).

49. Bread of heaven, fill me till I want no more, in the name

of Jesus.

50. Let all catering equipment of evil caterers attached to me be destroyed, in Jesus' name.

51. I command my digestive system to reject every evil command, in the name of Jesus.

52. Let all satanic designs of oppression against me in dreams and visions be frustrated, in Jesus' name.

53. I remove my name from the register of evil feeders with the blood of Jesus.

54. Let the habitation of evil caterers become desolate, in the name of Jesus.

55. I paralyse the spirits that bring bad dreams to me, in the name of Jesus.

56. Let the fire of the Holy Ghost destroy any evil list containing my name, in the name of Jesus.

57. Let the fire of the Holy Ghost destroy any of my photographs in the air, land and sea, in Jesus' name.

58. I destroy any coffin prepared for me, in Jesus' name.

59. I cancel and wipe off all evil dreams, in Jesus' name.

60. I destroy every satanic accident organised for my sake, in the name of Jesus.

61. I render all evil night creatures powerless, in the name of Jesus.

62. Let the blood of Jesus wash all the organs in my body, in the name of Jesus.

63. Let all sicknesses planted in my life through evil spiritual food be destroyed, in the name of Jesus.

64. Let the blood of Jesus erase all evil dreams in my life, in

Deliverance From Spirit Husband and Spirit Wife

the name of Jesus.

65. Let the fire of God boil all rivers harbouring unfriendly demons, in the name of Jesus.

66. Let all evil dreams be replaced with blessings, in the name of Jesus.

67. I command all my good dreams to come to pass, in the name of Jesus.

68. Father Lord, hasten the performance of my good dreams, in the name of Jesus.

8829558R00143

Printed in Great Britain
by Amazon.co.uk, Ltd.,
Marston Gate.